Managing Today's Schools

BRIDGING THEORY AND PRACTICE

This international series reflects the latest cutting-edge theories and practices in school leadership. Uniquely, we include books that bridge the perennial divide between theory and practice. The series motto is framed after Kurt Lewin's famous statement, and we paraphrase that there is no sound theory without practice and no good practice that is not framed on some theory.

Managing Today's Schools

New Skills for School Leaders in the 21st Century

Edited by Jeffrey Glanz

ROWMAN & LITTLEFIELD
Lanham • Boulder • New York • London

Published by Rowman & Littlefield
An imprint of The Rowman & Littlefield Publishing Group, Inc.
4501 Forbes Boulevard, Suite 200, Lanham, Maryland 20706
www.rowman.com

86-90 Paul Street, London EC2A 4NE

Copyright © 2022 by Jeffrey Glanz

All rights reserved. No part of this book may be reproduced in any form or by any electronic or mechanical means, including information storage and retrieval systems, without written permission from the publisher, except by a reviewer who may quote passages in a review.

British Library Cataloguing in Publication Information Available

Library of Congress Cataloging-in-Publication Data Available

ISBN: 978-1-4758-6248-5 (cloth)
ISBN: 978-1-4758-6249-2 (paper)
ISBN: 978-1-4758-6250-8 (electronic)

Contents

Series Editor's Introduction   vii
   Jeffrey Glanz

Editor's Introduction   1

1 Leading and Managing the School Organization with a Moral Purpose   7
   Clair T. Berube & Maurice R. Berube

2 Managing the Change Process through Teacher Empowerment: A New Role for the 21st-Century School Manager-Leader   23
   Shmuel Shenhav & Michael Reichel

3 Supporting Technology Integration in Schools: In Pursuit of New Skills for School Managers in the Post-Pandemic Era   37
   Köksal Banoğlu & Sedat Gümüş

4 Basic Principles of Teacher Evaluation Examined for School Leaders in the 21st Century   51
   Helen M. Hazi

5 Managing School Safety: Boundary Management within a Bourdieu Framework   63
   Pascale Benoliel

6 Leading the School Organization in the Evolving 21st-Century Legal Environment   79
   R. Stewart Mayers

7	Leadership for Flourishing: Positive Approaches to Relationship Building *Benjamin Kutsyuruba*	93
8	Fiscal Management: Guidelines for School Leaders *Leonard H. Elovitz*	109
9	Best Practices in School Management: A Multi-Dimensional Perspective *Jeffrey Glanz*	125

Index	137
About the Editor & Contributors	139

Series Editor's Introduction
Jeffrey Glanz

Why another book series on school leadership, and what does this particular series have to offer among the many fine books already published in the field of school and educational leadership?

Research over the past decade has confirmed what many educators, policymakers, think tanks, and others viscerally knew—that leadership makes a difference for a host of dependent variables, including the most important one, student achievement. Additional research is needed, however, to more fully refine and uncover how school leaders make a difference in a host of other areas.

The answers to additional research questions will offer further legitimacy and draw greater attention to the field of educational leadership. The questions (which can prompt potential authors to submit a book proposal) include the following, among others:

- What are the relationships among personal beliefs, identity, and leadership?
- What do the continuing increased accountability and high-stakes testing have on teacher morale, principal self-efficacy, and student achievement?
- What additional information do we need about systems thinking and its relationship to school leadership?
- What are the specific gender differences related to leading schools?
- How might school leaders remain proactive in educational reform?
- What is the precise role played by school leaders in fostering inclusive educational practices?
- How is justice and equity for all best fostered by school leaders?
- What specific educational leadership strategies reduce the Black/White achievement gap?

- What can we learn from studying educational leadership from a multidisciplinary perspective?
- What role does leadership style have on effectiveness as a leader?
- How might school leaders implement an effective data-driven decision-making process in their schools?
- What are the critical factors affecting high performance among principals?
- What is the role of school leaders in reducing school violence?
- How do leadership practices positively influence school-community-university partnerships?
- What is the association between transformational leadership and teacher self-efficacy?
- How does shared leadership affect school morale and productivity?
- How do various types or forms of leadership impact organizational effectiveness?
- What are the social, cultural, political, and historical factors that influence the practice of educational leadership in different countries?
- How do leadership practices differ in differing contexts, social, cultural, or otherwise?
- What are the theoretical and practical differences among educational administration, management, supervision, and leadership?
- Why is an international perspective so critical for better understanding the challenges of leading schools in the 21st century?
- How can school leaders address race and identity, bias and privilege, and racialized current events?
- How can comparative research studies help us better understand educational leadership?
- What can we learn from studying educational leaders beyond the school level (e.g., district and Ministry of Education leaders)?
- To what extent does emotional labor impact educational leaders?
- How can principals encourage action research, and other alternatives to supervision to enhance teacher professional growth?
- How do school leaders effectively implement new technologies not just for the sake of technology but to deepen learning and provide better support for teachers?
- What are the consequences of workload on school leaders (e.g., the principal, or others) on effectiveness as a leader?
- What are the challenges that school leaders face in differing regional contexts?
- How do school leaders develop the skills and knowledge they need to understand teachers' and students' needs and effectively guide learning?

- How do effective school leaders balance administrative duties with instructional priorities?
- What new educational management strategies can help teachers better confront classroom behavioral issues?
- How do school leaders coordinate curriculum and instructional initiatives across schools?
- Given time and budget constraints, how can school leaders find the resources to support artful education (music, dance, creative writing, etc.) for all students?
- How do increased efforts to promote teacher leadership impact the work of principals and their assistants?
- What new innovative ideas can principals implement to deal with the increasingly complex landscape of curriculum today?
- How can principals support teacher-led professional development?
- What is the role of identity in fostering principal self-efficacy?
- How can school leaders help schools become more integral to their surrounding communities—and how can they better leverage community resources and connections to support their students and teachers?
- How can we better balance interest and work in instructional leadership with other important leadership responsibilities?
- How can districts support assistant principals and prepare new principals as they take the helm of the school?
- How do we recruit, induct, and sustain good principals?
- How can we best prepare future school leaders?

The Series motto is framed after Kurt Lewin's famous statement, and I paraphrase, that there is no sound theory without practice and no good practice that is not framed on some theory. Most fundamentally, Bridging Theory and Practice: The Rowman & Littlefield School Leadership Series is premised on the need to connect theory to practice. Each of the questions above relies on a sound theoretical base that has important, if not critical relevance to the world of practice. This international series, in other words, reflects the latest cutting-edge theories and practices in school leadership that attempt to bridge the perennial divide between theory and practice.

Although we look to publish manuscripts that have relevance to an international audience, we will accept more localized research that might only be applicable in a specific context. We also encourage individuals who have completed a dissertation on a relevant topic to consider transforming their thesis into a book. Personally, my first book was framed on my dissertation, and I recall that the process was not so simple. If you think your work would have a larger appeal, I encourage you to consider a book with us. The manuscript, of course, must meet the rigors of academic research and address its possible impact on practice.

I welcome readers to join the effort to increase knowledge in our field and affect daily school practice by submitting a proposal on any of the topics mentioned above, or any other relevant ones. Feel free to communicate with me via email at yosglanz@gmail.com.

The Series is sponsored and supported by two important people. Special acknowledgment is extended to Thomas Koerner, Ph.D. (Vice President and Senior Executive Editor. Education Division for Rowman & Littlefield Publishers, Inc. Publisher for Education Issues) for his prompt feedback and encouragement. Special thanks to Kira Hall, Assistant Editor, for her expertise and support. Thanks to Madeline Kogler, Assistant Editor, for guiding the final production of this book with patience. With their assistance, I hope this Series will receive wide acknowledgment for making a difference in the field of educational leadership.

BOOKS ALREADY PUBLISHED IN THE SERIES

Brown, K. (2011). *Preparing future leaders for social justice, equity, and excellence: Bridging theory and practice through a transformative andragogy* (1st ed.). Rowman & Littlefield.

Brown, K., & Shaked, H. (2018). *Preparing future leaders for social justice: Bridging theory and practice through a transformative andragogy* (2nd ed.). Rowman & Littlefield.

Glanz, J. (Ed.). (2021). *Crisis and pandemic leadership: Implications for meeting the needs of students, teachers, and parents.* Rowman & Littlefield.

Stader, D. (2012). *Leadership for a culture of school safety: Linking theory to practice.* Rowman & Littlefield.

Zepeda, S. J. (Ed.). (2018). *Making learning job-embedded: Cases from the field of educational leadership.* Rowman & Littlefield.

Zepeda, S. J. (Ed.). (2018). *The job-embedded nature of coaching: Lessons and insights for school leaders.* Rowman & Littlefield.

Zepeda, S. J. (Ed.). (2008). *Real world supervision: Adapting theory to practice.* Rowman & Littlefield.

Editor's Introduction

As Series Editor, I am excited to introduce a book in which I am serving as the editor: *Managing Today's Schools: New Skills for School Leaders in the 21st Century*. This volume is distinguished from others in at least three ways: One, there are not many books singly devoted to school management. If one searches any of the book websites, one is hard-pressed to find a book singly devoted to school management. Most work on school management is part of larger works on school administration. Two, the fact that we focus on managerially operating a school, does not obviate the fact that contributors are aware and discuss the interconnectedness between management and leadership. Few, if any, books do so. Three, emphasis is placed on 21st-century cutting-edge ideas about school management.

Managing schools well today is more critical than ever. In thinking about managing a school today, we can draw upon true and tested ideas and skills of the past, but, by themselves, they would be insufficient. Schools have changed and so have the demands on school leaders. Therefore, new thinking on the subject and a new set of skills, or at least a refinement of old ones, are critically important. I have gathered a diverse and talented group of contributors who have brought unique perspectives on managing schools in the 21st century on a variety of topics.

Technologies and the very fabric of the way instruction, for instance, is being delivered today has changed. Moreover, schools today, worldwide in most places, are more diverse than ever before with large numbers of immigrant populations. This demographic change has challenged administrators to create new strategic visions to effectively manage and lead their schools. Consequently, school leaders must look at a new set of skills to successfully manage their schools, overall, and in specific areas.

Also, one of the important differences among current conceptions of school management with those of the past, is that in the past a manager was very different from a leader. In fact, most principals of yesteryear, by in large, saw their role as a manager first and foremost. The idea, for instance, of a principal serving as a teacher of teachers, involved in pedagogical or instructional leadership was uncommon, if not non-existent. Principals were hired primarily for their expertise in managing an organization. Hence, most of their time was spent on managing school operations. The notion of leadership, as distinct from management, didn't come on the scene, for the most part, until many years later. Still, when leadership was heralded as an essential task of a principal, a clear separation in functions between leadership and management was evident and practiced. Evidencing such bifurcation in emphases is the fact that journals we have today such as *School Leadership and Management* or *Educational Management, Administration, and Leadership* were unheard of decades ago.

In contrast to the previous century, successful principals today need both sets of skills (management and leadership), and they are not considered dichotomous. In other words, the differences between the two today are blurred. Both are crucial for the work of principals in the 21st century. Principals must affirm that both leadership and management are essential to achieve success in all facets of running a school. One is not necessarily more important than the other. An instructional leader cannot effectuate positive results without mindful attention to areas of management that support instructional goals and objectives. Principals who only view their roles as managers will often neglect other very important leadership-based school initiatives.

In this light, schools need to hire principals who, at once, realize the import of both functions, and have the requisite skills and experiences that support best practices in, for example, instructional leadership and school management. Some refer to this conception as seeing the two as two sides of one coin. Others see them as two halves of a one-sided coin. I, as editor of this volume, prefer the latter metaphor because it communicates more starkly the co-dependent nature of both. I sought chapter contributors who, essentially, share this vision.

Allow me to say a few words about each of the contributions. In chapter 1, Clair and Maurice Berube set the tone for the book by framing a perspective from which to view and understand school management as a moral enterprise. Previous works have highlighted the importance of school leadership from an ethical/moral perspective, but not so for school management. The latter has been traditionally seen operationally and perfunctorily. Yet, the authors of this opening chapter understand that such a view is short-sighted and detrimental to 21st-century schooling. Managing a school in inextricably entwined with its leadership counterpart. They make the case and provide realistic case studies to prompt thinking on the issue.

Shmuel Shenhav and Michael Reichel, in chapter 2, make the case for managing the ever-changing climate of 21st-century schooling through teacher empowerment. Drawing upon an intriguing concept from the business world, the authors discuss a concept known as "reverse management." They argue that it is a unique and valuable lens in which the principal becomes the manager or architect of the school environment to ensure mechanisms are in place so that teachers can take the lead in a variety of decision-making capacities. Their major contribution is that principals should be viewed as leader-managers who believe that schools today are too complex for one person "to do it all." They offer some practical advice to effectively navigate through the challenging, and sometimes troubling issues that confront modern schooling.

Köksal Banoğlu and Sedat Gümüş, in the next chapter, address the role of technology in the day-to-day practices of school managers. Technology is obviously a big issue in 21st-century schooling, especially in the post-pandemic era. The authors frame their chapter based on the existing international literature and provide a list of suggestions for school managers to implement information and communication technology (ICT) in their efforts to manage the school. Their unique contribution, however, is that they address the use of ICT in a dual manner. They highlight its benefit in promoting ICT integration in teaching and learning activities, but also connect it to operational management.

Helen M. Hazi, in chapter 4, demonstrates that school management is not merely relegated to the periphery of the instructional process. Rather, principals play a critical role in managing the learning process for teachers in the 21st century. She offers principles for teacher evaluation that are relevant for a changing the educational landscape in the 21st century. She charges that it is high-time educators get teacher evaluation right. She states that principals should ensure that teachers "have a seat at the table" in terms of managing their own professional growth in learning. This imperative requires skillful management and creative leadership, working hand-in-hand to promote excellence in teaching and meaningful student learning. Again, this chapter, along with every other one in *Managing Today's Schools: New Skills for School Leaders in the 21st Century* conceives and views management and leadership as integral partners, if you will, in the effective and efficient operation of all facets of a school.

In a chapter entitled "Managing School Safety: Boundary Management within a Bourdieu Framework," Pascale Benoliel contributes an intellectually engaging discussion drawing on the work of famed French philosopher, Pierre Bourdieu. Drawing on his theoretical framework and accompanying concepts, she integrates them with organizational structures, policies, and procedures to encourage principals to implement school-specific procedures for school safety. Concretely, she emphasizes the importance of building relationships with external stakeholders to promote school safety in its various dimensions. By engaging in internal and external boundary activities, principals can manage the school safety issue with alacrity.

In chapter 6, R. Stewart Mayers highlights several key 21st-century legal issues that have direct implications on managing schools in the new century. He draws upon the Title VII employment discrimination protection issues, technology-driven changes in speech and search law, as well as current issues in Title IX of the Education Amendments of 1972. He argues for continued professional development to prepare principals with the tools for managing incidents that implicate the legal system. These skills, he says, include proper planning for specific situations and having appropriate policies in place to support the school's preparation to deal with these situations. School leaders also need a basic knowledge of the law and the legal system to react appropriately, advise other employees on their actions, and provide needed information and artifacts to the district's legal counsel.

In the next chapter, Benjamin Kutsyuruba discusses the importance of building relationships (so that a school can "flourish") as integral to leading a school with manifest implications for school management. The chapter describes findings from a research study that examined perceptions of flourishing in the work lives of national award-winning principals in the Canada's Outstanding Principals (COP) program. After providing a strong theoretical background, findings and implications for practice are offered. Readers are encouraged, in the case study, to apply the research to practically moving a dysfunctional school into one that is flourishing.

The next to last chapter in *Managing Today's Schools: New Skills for School Leaders in the 21st Century*, Leonard H. Elovitz addresses a critical and necessary component of any work on school management—finances. He explores the financial skills necessary for school leaders to be successful at both the district and school levels. In a sort of primer for any principal who wants to successfully manage a school, he reviews practical questions any manager would ask and needs to know: "Where does the money that will be used to manage the school come from?"; "How is the money allocated?"; and "How will and should it be spent?" He also discusses practical ways to expand resources beyond the traditional and usual outlets.

In the final chapter, I discuss practical strategies for school managers in four areas: managing the school organization, coordinating and overseeing school facilities, highlighting school budget issues, and managing human relations. The chapter emphasizes the importance of viewing the work of principals from both a leadership and management perspective, simultaneously. In this light, schools need to hire principals who have the requisite skills and experiences and can, at once, realize the import of both functions. Managing schools in the 21st century is more complicated than ever.

Finally, to encourage readers to introspect regarding issues presented, each chapter includes case study-type scenarios, in various formats, with thought-provoking questions to, at once, summarize the ideas of the chapter, and to help readers think about ways they might put the ideas of the chapter into practice.

I encourage readers to correspond with our contributors to further deepen the conversation about the role of management in schools. We welcome your feedback and participation.

Jeffrey Glanz
February 2022

Chapter One

Leading and Managing the School Organization with a Moral Purpose

Clair T. Berube & Maurice R. Berube

INTRODUCTION

Leadership is a most overused and misunderstood concept. It is not management, but it cannot exist without it. This chapter is premised on the amalgamation of both leadership and management. In other words, the two concepts in the 21st century not merely co-exist but are dependent on one another. Schools without efficient and effective management cannot achieve optimal functioning, nor can they maximize moral vision without mindful and values-based leadership. In the past, they were conceived, at best, as two sides of one coin. A more accurate, even necessary, idiom or conception is that, in essence, they cannot be separated but must be viewed as working in conjunction with one another without superficial or arbitrary boundaries, even though they each have different foci. Both, however, must be moral.

Leadership, at its core, is visionary and creative. It is motivational and inspirational. It perceives beyond organization and effective performance. It is an idea that by its very nature is moral; it achieves a good. In the domain of K–12 education, effective leadership must include a moral element, or else the individual student is sacrificed at the expense of regulations, or testing, or standardized paper-pushing bureaucrats. Conversely, management of the organization must fulfill its moral obligations by establishing a framework conducive to and supportive of student learning.

Often in education, scholars studying leadership will focus exclusively on the school or district organization without mindful attention to the imperative of moral leadership, Similarly, scholarship on school management is often devoid of attention to moral leadership. What is moral leadership and how does it interface with and operate within the school organization? What do they look like in practical terms in schools? This chapter will examine moral K–12 leadership and management as they pertain to the following questions:

- Can effective moral school leaders hold high standards, ensuring that all students' needs are met and create a holistic warm, and equitable school climate and culture?
- Can effective moral school leaders inspire both faculty and students to achieve their highest potential, and in doing so, realize the vision of the leader?
- Can effective moral school leaders model values in the Deweyan (1966) sense to ensure that all students are well-rounded, knowledgeable, and caring citizens?
- And finally, having set the moral tone of the school, how does management look like a part of the moral culture at the classroom and building level?

The authors of this chapter will use these questions as frameworks toward an understanding of what it takes to effectively lead a school with a moral and ethical purpose. The review of the literature will help explain how other scholars have framed moral and ethical leadership, and the chapter will conclude with a discussion with three K–12 leaders chosen by the authors as real-world practical case studies of such moral leadership.

THEORETICAL BACKGROUND

Schools as Moral Institutions

It has been suggested that colleges and universities are moral institutions by their very natures and definitions (Berube & Berube, 2010). They have a moral responsibility to the faculty, students, and local communities in which they are situated. The philosophy and culture of the institution, whether it be a college or a public K–12 school, as is the case in this chapter, set the tone for everything that takes place in the school. To begin, there must be a working definition of what "moral" means as it pertains to education. According to the Cambridge dictionary, moral means "relating to the standards of good or bad behavior, fairness, honesty, etc. that each person believes in, rather than laws" (Cambridge Dictionary, n.d.).

This is a very important definition because it speaks to the importance of the individual student or person who, in a moral environment, is placed above rules in importance. Rules can be unjust, but morality is at a higher level than the idea of a rule-based culture. This is not to say that schools should be without rules; on the contrary, moral rules are the bedrock of all successful institutions. However, many times rules are abused as a means towards an end at the expense of the individual context of the situation. Is it ever a good idea to sacrifice a person's spirit and soul for the gain of a principle that may be flawed?

An example of this would be the zero-tolerance craze that ignores individual circumstances and opportunities for a growth model when dealing with human behavior. The kindergartener who gets expelled for bringing nail clippers to a school that has a zero-tolerance weapons policy would be such an example. Or the fight between two boys on the playground, where punches are exchanged. The boys show up bloodied and scruffy in the principal's office. The rule could say that fist fights automatically result in suspension, which means several days of lost instruction; or the principal could have the boys talk to each other and shake hands to resolve the situation in a more nuanced and humanistic way. Some principals won't even bother to find out the reason for the fight because the more expedient approach is simply to suspend them both.

The example above lacks a moral core. Moral leaders place events into context; taking the harder-to-do approach and working to find what is going on. Moral leaders look at the whole child when dealing with situations such as these. The most effective school leaders maintain very high standards while at the same time treating faculty and students as individual humans worthy of learning from mistakes (growth models).

What questions or guidelines should administrators consider as they prepare to lead a K–12 institution? Experts in this field each have their lists of guidelines. Lynch (2015) lists eight principles of ethical leadership in education. These include personal courage (to stand up to policies they feel are not helpful to their students); public interest ahead of self (the needs of students and staff must come before needs of administrator); self-control, self-discipline, and integrity (be a positive role model); task and employee centeredness (focus on needs of employees and staff); recognizing talent (using each staff member to allow strengths to shine); requiring high ethics from everyone (including staff, parents, shareholders, etc.); sensitivity and understanding (political, economic, cultural, to create an inclusive community as evidenced by policies); and inclusiveness (a sense of belonging and respect for all involved) (para. 3–11 on the website).

The National Association of Secondary School Principals (NASSP, 2021) has their list of recommendations for school leaders:

1. Makes the well-being and success of students the fundamental value in all decision-making and actions.
2. Fulfills professional responsibilities with honesty and integrity.

3. Supports the principle of due process and protects the civil and human rights of all individuals.
4. Obeys local, state, and federal laws.
5. Implements the governing board of education's policies and administrative rules and regulations.
6. Pursues appropriate measures to correct those laws, policies, and regulations that are not consistent with sound educational goals.
7. Avoids using positions for personal gain through political, social, religious, economic, or other influence.
8. Accepts academic degrees or professional certification only from duly accredited institutions.
9. Maintains the standards of and seeks to improve the effectiveness of the profession through research and continuing professional development.
10. Honors all contracts until fulfillment, release, or dissolution mutually agreed upon by all parties to contract (para. 4 on the website).

Interestingly, this list of recommendations does indeed include a stipulation that the leader will pursue measures to correct unjust or immoral rules, which is the number one moral consideration necessary for ethical leadership according to the authors of this chapter. Sometimes leaders and administrators (managers) value absolute "justice" (based on human-made rules) over "goodness" during decision-making. This in turn can create the zero-tolerance cases we hear about so often in the news today. The inspirational and motivational aspect of school leadership is crucial in creating a moral culture in a school.

Leadership with a Moral Purpose

Leadership by its very definition includes a moral aspect, however in the social sciences wherein humans are the currency, moral leadership is at its most important application. One of the main reasons the authors either earned degrees in urban studies and education or worked in urban education was to fulfill the moral obligation of being educators. Public education is the best vehicle for democracy America has ever known, and it is imperative that all students have access to this ladder towards the American Dream. Unfortunately, in the course of U.S. history, many of those in power have purposefully undermined public education to perpetuate a permanent underclass of Americans, thereby stripping them of the ability to climb the ladder into the middle class. One of the tenets of moral leadership is to ensure that there is equity to provide each student with the equal opportunities afforded them by law. This speaks to the culture and environment of the school and building.

Among the leading researchers in educational moral leadership has been Michael Fullan, a Canadian educational researcher on school reform, and Global Leadership Director, New Pedagogies for Deep Learning. In his book *The Moral Imperative of School Leadership*, Fullan (2003) argues that good school leaders; those who have a moral higher purpose, create a contextual environment where students and faculty can *be* more moral. If the leader creates a culture where the details of a student's life is important and sets up a structure where these "little things" matter, then everyone will have a space in which to be more moral. Fullan (as stated in Gladwell, 2000) mentions that "in order to change people's beliefs, one needs to create a community around them where these new beliefs could be practical, expressed and nurtured" (Fullan, 2003, p. 2). Fullan goes on to state that change cannot happen at the individual level at first; that a leader has to change the culture of the school for morality to thrive. According to Fullan:

> You don't have to go very far into the question of the role of public schools in a democracy before discovering that moral purpose is at the heart of the matter. The best case for public education has always been that is a common good. Everyone, ultimately, has a stake in the caliber of schools, and education is everyone's business. The quality of the public education system relates directly to the quality of life that people enjoy (whether as parents, employers, or citizens), with a strong public education system as the cornerstone of a civil, prosperous, and democratic society. As the main institution for fostering social cohesion in an increasingly diverse society, publicly funded schools must serve all children, not simply those with the loudest or most powerful advocates. This means addressing the cognitive and social needs of all children, with an emphasis on including those who may not have been well served in the past. For instance, a focus on academic achievement, such as improving literacy and mathematics, must include a commitment to narrowing the gap between high- and low-achieving children. (p. 3)

If principals, despite external pressures, are only worried about the results of annual standardized high stakes test scores and not about the moral culture of the school, then a vital part of schooling is awry. Making an effort to close these educational gaps is in itself a moral endeavor. Fullan (2002) discusses how principals can demonstrate a moral purpose with students:

> School leaders with a moral purpose seek to make a difference in the lives of students. They are concerned about closing the gap between high-performing and lower-performing schools and raising the achievement of—and closing the gap between—high-performing and lower-performing students. They act with the intention of making a positive difference in their own schools as well as improving the environment in other district schools. (p. 17)

Most importantly, Fullan (2002) argues that most "change" is superficial and structural. He suggests that transforming the culture of the school by changing what people in the organization value and how they work together to secure the change, is what really results in deep and lasting change (p. 18). How, though, does a principal effect cultural change at the building level? What do this moral culture and climate look like?

Schools as the Community

As organizations, school managers, similarly, have moral responsibilities towards the communities that they serve. Not only are schools a part of the community, but they are also the community. Neighborhood schools are the anchors in all neighborhoods. The fight for neighborhood schools is critical for just this reason. The privatization of public schools has been an ongoing battle for years now, with a push towards charter schools as being the perceived savior of the public education system. Charters are in reality public schools that have extra funding and do not have to enroll everyone that applies. Aside from the fact that charter schools are no better than a decent public neighborhood school, the problem with charter schools is that they are neighborhood school killers. If a neighborhood school is disrupted, the bedrock of that neighborhood is morally transformed.

What have been the results of charter schools? Berube (2014) explained:

> As far as measurable, quantitative results, a scandal was uncovered in 2004. The federal government had tested a sample of American charter schools in 2003, but did not release the findings when it was supposed to in November 2004, when other results were released for states and the nation. They were uncovered on the federal testing agencies website by staff members of the American Federation of Teachers (AFT). Results showed that NAEP (National Assessment of Educational Progress; "Nation's Report Card"), "showed no measurable differences on tests of reading and mathematics between fourth-grade students from similar racial/ethnic backgrounds in charter schools and in regular public schools. Among poor students, fourth graders in regular public schools outperformed those in charter schools in both subjects. (pp. 65, 66)

If outcomes are not the point of charter schools, then what is? According to Jonathan Kozol (2005), it is re-segregation. Charter schools do not by law have to enroll students that they do not want to be enrolled. This means that charters engage in something called "cream-skimming" where they look through their applicants (access gained through a lottery) and choose whom they want. Meanwhile, down the street, the neighborhood public school must by law admit everyone and do not get the luxury of admitting only the best and most motivated and then reporting what a wonderful school they are. Kozol states:

> 'Choice, left to itself,' he said, 'will increase stratification. Nothing in the way choice systems actually work favors class or racial integration,' . . . As for the current trend toward charter schools, which represent one form of choice, he noted that 'most charter schools are more intensely segregated than the average public school, not less . . . ,' and he argued firmly against charter schools and other programs of school choice that do not have specific stipulations that will lessen segregation rather than increase it. (225, 226)

It is a moral imperative that schools educated everyone at the public-school level. Charter schools are not the solution and are a distraction towards applying what we know works in schools and using this to fix neighborhood public schools.

Control over the Neighborhood School

One of the authors of this chapter (M. Berube) was instrumental in the community control movement in New York City in 1968. He worked for the Center for Urban Studies at Queens College and with the Director, Marilyn Gittell, wrote a seminal book of the movement entitled *Confrontation at Ocean Hill—Brownsville; the New York school strikes of 1968* (Berube & Gittell, 1969). 57,000 New York City teachers went on strike in protest of the local African American community gaining control of the school district Ocean Hill—Brownsville; a low-income African American district in Brooklyn. An experiment was playing out where parents and community activists were given control over their local schools. New York City public school teachers were transferred out of the district or to other schools while teachers of the new board's choosing were put into place.

This raised the hackles of the American Federation of Teachers, led by Albert Shanker and they did have a point. Most of the transferred teachers were of the Jewish faith who had good intentions and loved their jobs. They were good teachers and very dedicated to their work. Many of them crossed picket lines to continue to serve the students. However, the parents in the district also had a point and wanted a more representative faculty in place and a say in the curriculum. While not permanently successful, the experiment brought to the surface the moral questions of who should teach our children? What body of work (the Canon) should our children be taught? How is culture left out of public education? Who should be running our schools? It is the moral duty of a public-school administrator to address these questions.

This theoretical background has laid the basis for schools as moral institutions, for its leaders as having a moral imperative, and has inferred that schools must be managed with moral purpose.

PRACTICAL APPLICATIONS OF MORAL K–12 LEADERSHIP AND MANAGEMENT

Three Case Studies

In seeking answers to the questions posed in the Introduction and to concretize the discussion in this chapter, the authors interviewed three K–12 Virginia public and private school principals whom they deemed as possessing morally sound leadership and management capacities. The principals were sent a set of questions and then the answers were coded using qualitative research design techniques (Miles et al., 2014) to discover trends and similarities. Each principal case study was organized according to coded themes that emerged from the data. The following case studies used a coded name as well as real names with permission.

All three of these leaders have exceptional interpersonal abilities, very high emotional quotients (EQ), and the courage to fulfill moral obligations. They are each stellar examples of principals who love and care for their educational communities and who create nurturing and supportive working and learning environments. Sometimes, themes overlapped. We noted the highlights of each principal's responses and some of these crossed over to other categories. The themes that emerged are found in the underlined text below. Parenthetically, we gathered much data but will only report on ideas related, directly or indirectly, to the four questions posed in the Introduction.

Case #1

The first administrator is a retired principal with 26 years in various local (Southeastern Virginia) public school divisions. As a female person of color, she is a caring and a spiritual individual who looks for the good in everyone and keeps a firm handle on moral development and principles guiding her leadership and management styles. She has held several leadership positions; both at the K–12 and University level and is constantly called upon to contribute her knowledge and expertise.

Fairness and alternative approaches to discipline: "School/classroom discipline is an organized program [well-managed] that assists students' adjustment to the fact that every action, good or bad, has consequences. This was especially important in my school settings because many students came from homes where there were no consequences or they were heavily punished for them (the punishment does not fit the behavior). What schools should desire is to discipline by teaching positive replacements for the bad behavior and not punitive actions which many students are used to."

People skills: "I worked diligently at building the right relationships so that we could work together for the success of the students. I held many parent workshops, proposed grants for families and schools working together, and created a family-friendly environment in the building. I realized that there always needed to be compassion and forgiveness shown especially when it was in my power to do so. When dealing with people I did it from the heart. I believed that each person that I met had a purpose in my life and deserved a smile and kind words. I really loved interacting with people and learning something from everyone I met."

School climate/culture: "Given the opportunity and proper support and resources, every child can grow instructionally while learning digital, social, and emotional skills. Every school needs to encourage high-level content while promoting opportunities using culturally diverse pedagogy in classrooms."

Teacher development/Growth model: "Various kinds of assessments can assist in ways teachers can improve performance. I was able to do this through professional development for faculty. Faculty members at my school were encouraged to write proposals to try new ideas and for student growth as long as it did not hinder or threaten student success in any way. As a result, I would financially support and monitor the projects."

Case #2

The second administrator is Steven Hammond. From 1979 to the present, Steve has served in various administrative capacities in Catholic and independent schools including the roles of elementary, middle, and high schools building principal, central office curriculum director, school president, and superintendent of schools. In the last 25 years, he has worked with various boards and starting school programs. He has helped start six schools. Steve currently works as the founding Principal at Saint Patrick Catholic School in Norfolk, Virginia. He follows a progressive education model based on John Dewey's (1966) educating the whole child, and William Glasser's (1999) theory of human behavior called Choice Theory. Mr. Hammond's school is a relaxed, caring, and supportive place with extremely high standards but wherein fear cannot be found and where people are encouraged to be themselves.

Fairness: "Justice can be seen through the lens of fairness as in judging behavior based upon an agreed-upon set of standards and/or equity which suggests that all members will be treated equally. Of course, if equitable treatment is part of the agreed-upon standards, a behavior management system is obliged to take into account both of these means, fairness, and equity, make up its definition of justice."

Alternative approaches to discipline: "I do not believe that radical behaviorism, the work of B. F. Skinner (1974), or the mini forms of behavior modification stemming from Skinner's thought are usually the most effective forms of school discipline. This is not to say that it does not work for many people but it is to say that oftentimes harms individuals in varying ways, sometimes for a lifetime. A cognitive-behavioral approach with children which eliminates punishment or reward is by far a better approach for most students, 7 years old and up, if delivered in an age-appropriate manner. . . . I prefer to work with students and youth not through external power, but through the process of student reflection, restorative justice, planning for improvement and implementing that plan over time."

Individual context/common sense: "I am a minimalist. I prefer to [manage by] having as few rules and regulations as is possible. In this way, the school is not backed into a corner pro forma and can better deal with individual situations appropriately. I believe that schools need the latitude to address individual issues uniquely and thoroughly. Having a static set of punishments or behavior responses for individual actions has never made a lot of sense to me. In this system, equity is not the driving force because the response to the student's misbehavior may vary widely from student to student. The system is fair, however, because the community knows that the school will deal with behavior issues on a one-to-one basis."

People skills: "If the school chooses to establish a culture that is built upon hospitality, respect, empathy, and quality, then it feels good to be inside the community. If a school chooses to use collaborative, democratic problem-solving as much as possible, then people know that their voices are respected and valued. Undoubtedly there should be norms that outline the rights and duties of all stakeholders in the community. However, a school can have all the appropriate, well-written handbooks in the world but without goodwill, relationships will fall apart. Based on my experiences, great leadership is highly relational. Developing relationships can come about in many different ways, but to be sure, there has to be a meaningful, dynamic relationship between the leader and those s/he is leading."

School climate/culture: "Great leaders are loyal to their staff and will have their back if needed. This does not mean that they will justify poor or unacceptable behavior, but they will not allow their staff to be bullied or victimized. Great leaders are great problem solvers who form teams, collaborate, develop strategic plans, and implement them to successful completion. Great leaders give their staff the credit for successful work and accept responsibility when things do not go well. They praise in public and address individual problems in private. Great leaders delegate well and interest staff in doing superior work. These leaders emphasize high quality and ask their staff to develop plans, personal plans to achieve it.

Let them know that your office door is open to them and encourage them to just drop in to visit, and likewise, drop into their classes from time to time just to hang out. Let them know you care about them and deeply appreciate the fantastic job they are doing. These things can spawn growth, . . . oftentimes more than what takes place in an accreditation or evaluation cycle. If a school chooses to use collaborative, democratic problem solving as much as possible, then people know that their voices are respected and valued. A school can establish ground rules or guidelines that indicate that criticizing blaming and complaining is not part of the school culture and if anyone has a problem, address it to the individuals who can best facilitate a solution. All children, in fact, all human beings need to be loved and to be valued. Teachers at all levels should communicate establish a classroom environment where these are communicated to every student."

Case #3

The third administrator, Bob Grant, is a retired Principal and former Assistant Principal at public urban middle schools in Norfolk, Virginia, and at a private military academy, also in Virginia. Dr. Grant was one of the superiors of C. Berube at the beginning of her career when she served as a middle school science teacher at Blair Middle School, Norfolk Virginia. Dr. Grant had the ear of parents and students and was the "warm/fuzzy" administrator who used great people skills along with a giant sense of humor to accomplish good things. He was a much-loved Assistant Principal and solved many problems through his superior people skills.

Fairness, alternative approaches to discipline: "I tried to make sure that school and class rules made sense and were fair to all concerned. Of course, some were not under the control of the school-level administrator, but many were. I tried to use out-of-school suspension only as a last resort or for serious offenses (fighting, etc.) and even developed a "Saturday School" program as an alternative punishment to out of school suspension. I feel that the development of self-discipline is one of the main tasks of schools, and rules/regulations and consequences can assist in this with young people."

Individual context/common sense: "I tried to be quick to intervene when I saw a problem (or it was brought to my attention) but always tried to be fair and consistent, and listened to the individual's explanation or point of view. Again, there were a couple of situations that were pretty automatic but for the most part I worked with the individual staff or student to correct the issue.

One time an LD (learning disabled) student had a family who ran a cattle farm. The security officers ran a check of cars in the student parking lot (though most of them were pick-up trucks!) and found a box cutter in this lad's truck. Of course, weapons were completely prohibited so he was suspended and recommended by the Superintendent for expulsion. Now part of this boy's family responsibilities was to stop at the fields on the way home from school and open bales of hay to feed the cattle . . . to him it was a tool and not a weapon. I argued on his behalf, but the Superintendent insisted that the Board expel him, which they did. I just felt that was totally unfair and against the spirit of the law."

People skills: "Although much of my people skills are perhaps just my personality, I also think the many years I spent as a school counselor contributed to what I feel are good people skills. I am a good listener, a positive thinker, and always look for how I can help out the other person. This was always my approach to students and teachers alike. I love being with other people (which has made the pandemic restrictions very difficult for me) always try to find a way to bring humor into the situation and try to end every situation on a positive note.

When it comes to my treatment of students, I am definitely more likely to err on the side of kindness. I don't expect the teachers to be perfect, but I always expected them to set a standard of excellence in everything they do that remotely involves the students."

School climate/culture: "While the principal is often referred to as the Instructional Leader of the school, which is, of course, true, I have always believed other aspects of the role are more important. The principal must do everything he or she can to ensure a warm and positive school climate. The students' overall growth and development are what is paramount in my opinion. I always insisted that my teachers treat their students as they would want their own children treated at school . . . anything was less was totally unacceptable. I was always the number one fan of my students (especially when successful) and the number one cheerleader for my teachers. I insisted that every adult try to establish a warm and positive relationship with as many students as possible as this is what makes school climate."

Growth model/Teacher development: "I involved the teachers in the development of their professional growth plans and constantly looked for opportunities for them. If an individual's performance fell short, we would together develop an improvement plan. As long as he or she was making progress toward the goal all was well. It was only if no improvement happened, or if it appeared that he or she was not trying or did not care that I would move in a disciplinary approach. Since I was always opposed to faculty meetings that were mere recitations of items that could be put in a memo/email I would try to plan some short professional growth activity from which all teachers could benefit from each faculty meeting. The implementation of these was then discussed by myself and the other administrators during post-observation conferences."

REFLECTION ON CASE STUDIES

1. How do the cases above demonstrate, if they do, leading and managing with a moral purpose? Explain.
2. What does leading and managing with a moral purpose mean to you?
3. Can you provide examples or models of leaders you know who have led and managed with moral purpose?

CONCLUSION

It is the opinion of the authors that there are traits moral leaders share, and many of them have been noted in this chapter, especially coming through in the qualitative data in the section above. Above-average people skills are at the top of the list, and along with that the emotional intelligence to persuade people to follow a principal's path and vision. Being a moral leader does not mean that the leader will never be angry, frustrated, or discouraged. Neither will the principal be able to circumvent all bureaucratic mandates (as in the example culled from Case #3 wherein the student was expelled). Rather it means that the moral leader always keeps in mind a higher purpose.

A good leader with a moral compass can take their team on a journey in their careers wherein they know without a doubt that their leader/manager has their best interests at heart and forges a moral vision for the school. A good moral leader will never use employees for their personal benefit, and at the employee's expense. A good moral leader will never demean, insult, micromanage, or demoralize their team. They operate on a democratic paradigm in which they hold high standards and do not bow to the whims of bureaucratic impositions.

A reading of the cases as a whole reflects that moral leaders hold high standards and nurture a people-oriented school culture (based on question 1 from the Introduction). Moral leaders are visionary and inspire both faculty and students (question 2). Moral leaders construct their philosophy of school management and leadership upon a Deweyan framework (question 3). And management of the school reflects the moral culture at the classroom and building levels (question 4).

An effective principal in the 21st century views school management and educational leadership through a moral lens. The father of American education – John Dewey (1966), summed it up best when he posited that the three characteristics of education are necessary for every child: intellectual development, social development, and moral development. Moral leadership and management theory rests on that crucible.

REFERENCES

Berube, C. (2014). *STEM and the city: A report on the STEM education in the great American urban public school system.* Information Age Publishing.

Berube, M., & Berube, C. (2010). *The moral university.* Rowman & Littlefield.

Berube, M., & Gittell, M. (1969). *Confrontation at Ocean Hill—Brownsville: The New York school strikes of 1968.* Praeger.

Cambridge Dictionary. (n.d.). Moral. In *Cambridge dictionary.* MORAL | meaning in the Cambridge English Dictionary.

Dewey, J. (1966). *Democracy and education: An introduction to the philosophy of education.* The Free Press.

Fullan, M. (2002). The change leader. *Educational Leadership, 59*(8), 16–20. http://www.ascd.org/publications/educational-leadership/may02/vol59/num08/The-Change-Leader.aspx.

Fullan, M. (2003). *The moral imperative of school leadership.* Corwin.

Gladwell, M. (2000). *The tipping point.* Little, Brown & Co.

Glasser, W. (1999). *Choice theory: A new psychology of personal freedom.* Harper Perennial.

Kozol, J. (2005). *The shame of the nation: The restoration of apartheid schooling in America.* Crown Publishers.

Lynch, M. (2015). The eight principles of ethical leadership in education, The Edvocate: Educational Leadership. The Eight Principles of Ethical Leadership in Education - The Edvocate (theedadvocate.org).

Miles M. B., Huberman, M.A., & Saldanila, J. (2014). *Qualitative data analysis: A methods sourcebook* (3rd ed.). SAGE.

National Association of Secondary School Principals (NASSP). (2021). *Ethics for school leaders.* NASSP.

Skinner, B. F. (1974). *About behaviorism.* Alfred A. Knopf.

Chapter Two

Managing the Change Process through Teacher Empowerment

A New Role for the 21st-Century School Manager-Leader

Shmuel Shenhav & Michael Reichel

INTRODUCTION

Early conceptions of school leadership and management focused on the idea that these were two distinct aspects of a principal's responsibilities. Both leadership and management were viewed as important, yet very different and sometimes even antagonistic to one another (Duffy, 2016). Such thinking has dramatically changed in the 21st century. Among the many reasons for a re-visioning of the two processes include the fact that schools today are very different from schools of yesteryear. The challenges school leaders face today have skyrocketed given the ever-changing educational, political, economic, social, and technological landscape. Principals, today, must simultaneously lead and manage a multitude of tasks.

The topic is broad, therefore, for purposes of this chapter, we will focus on the role of the principal in managing school change in instructional improvement by empowering teachers to assume greater authority for their work and development. In the past, given the authoritarian nature of top-down management, principals took sole responsibility for ensuring instructional improvement. Today, principals and teachers share in the management and leadership processes, with teachers assuming greater control over their work more than ever before. Both leadership and management in the 21st century are vital to empowering teachers to embrace change and to engage in their own instructional leadership initiatives.

The next section reviews some of the theory that supports the thinking underlying these aforementioned ideas. Understanding the changing landscape of educational change in the 21st century is critical to lead schools effectively. One of the more important changes involves the ever-increasing expectations for school leaders to become more actively involved in pedagogical or instructional leadership. A consequence of this development has been the rise in importance of increasing opportunities for classroom teachers to become more involved in curricular decisions, instructional leadership, and even participating in needed in-school reforms. Teacher autonomy finds likely justification by principals in their efforts to improve their school, especially in raising student achievement.

THEORETICAL BACKGROUND

The Changing Educational Landscape

21st-century schooling is dramatically different from anything that has come before. Given the increases in population coupled with the ever-changing and diverse student body, increase in digitalization and automation, the exponential advances in technology overall, and the impact of a global economy, schools and their principals are confronted with new and demanding challenges. The need to adapt schools, leadership, and teaching to meet 21st-century demands and expectations has been at the forefront of educational research and debate, especially over the last decade. Effecting major changes like schooling and instructional practices requires adopting new and often changing educational paradigms (Blass, 2018; Orakcı, 2020). However, changing educational paradigms and practices is not so simple (Kovacs, 2017), as school leaders must fight against both bureaucratic constraints (Shenhav et al., 2020) and teachers' inclination to teach as they were taught and behave as functionaries within the school bureaucracy. But these are the challenges of the 21st-century principal.

The success of educational change inevitably depends on the quality and performance of principals and other school leaders (Hallinger & Heck, 2011; Shaked, 2019). The importance of recruiting high-quality leaders and retaining them is widely acknowledged in the statements of policymakers (Jones & Ringler, 2020). The challenge, as always, is the ability to attract and retain effective school leaders who can manage their schools seamlessly (Stark et al., 2017).

Extant research and anecdotal evidence indicate that many schools have been unaffected by cutting-edge practices in instructional leadership. For instance, supervision of instruction in most schools is performed perfunctorily, utilizing traditional methods of evaluative supervision and episodic utilization of professional development. Research indicates that such practices do not encourage change in teacher behavior that results in student achievement

(Glickman et al., 2017). More specifically, extant research indicates that effective principals understand that:

1. The single greatest influence on students in a classroom is the teacher. "Teachers have a powerful, long-lasting influence on their students" (Stronge, 2007, p. vii). Good principals support good teachers by providing instructional services and resources continuingly, but also and equally important, to empower them by engaging them to take an active role in managing the instructional process.
2. Teacher autonomy is necessary to collaborate with teachers on school-wide instructional policies, to involve them in curricular decision-making, and to provide teachers with meaningful opportunities for professional growth (Blasé & Blasé, 2004).
3. Principals and other administrators work to develop a professional learning community (Sullivan & Glanz, 2006). A professional learning community has five dimensions: (1) supportive and shared leadership (e.g., school administrators participate democratically with teachers sharing power, authority, and decision-making); (2) shared values and vision (e.g., the principal and staff decide on the values and vision of the school and support its realization); (3) collective learning (e.g., staff and the administration come together to learn how best to improve student performance); (4) supportive conditions (e.g., principals and teachers possess adequate resources to promote instructional excellence and create structures that facilitate learning for all); and (5) shared personal practice (e.g., peer review and feedback are school norms as is feedback given to administrators by teachers in informal and formal ways) (Hord, 1997 as cited by Morrissey, 2000, pp. 4, 32–33).

So, we see that we need to recruit principals who fully realize the changing landscape of schooling in the 21st century. Moreover, they need the knowledge, skills, and dispositions to embrace and effect needed changes. The remainder of this review will highlight two changes that are critical if schools and their principals are to successfully navigate the demands of the 21st century: instructional or pedagogical leadership and teacher autonomy.

Meta-Leaders Embraces Instructional Leadership and Teacher Autonomy

Marcus, McNulty, Henderson, and Dorn (2019) at Harvard University explore meta-leadership as an effective framework for identifying a constructive view of school leadership in the 21st century. They explain that meta-leadership is viewed through the following three dimensions:

1. the *person* or personal characteristics of principals who exhibit emotional intelligence, and who develop credibility, trusting relationships [e.g., leaders who are ready and able to embrace the demands of schooling in the 21st century]
2. the *situation* and a principal's grasp of the complex problem and actions are taken through communication and decision-making [e.g., leaders who realize that instructional leadership is a necessary skill in the 21st century]
3. the *connectivity* and how principals build networks through partnerships, collaboration, and work with stakeholders [e.g., leaders who value teacher autonomy].

Marcus et al. (2019) refer to a leader who embodies the ideals above as a meta-leader. A meta-leader is a role model, who recognizes and embraces change, conflict, and crisis. They are leaders, above all, who when confronted with change "possess[es] a depth of emotional intelligence" (p. 106). Emotional intelligence is defined through framework as a leader who exhibits five key attributes (Goleman et al., 2002):

1. *Self-awareness:* the leader's understanding of self and what drives them. Self-aware leaders understand both their strengths and weaknesses.
2. *Self-regulation:* the leader's ability to control their moods, impulses, and interactions with others. Leaders who self-regulate can control their emotions and remain calm and level-headed.
3. *Motivation:* the leader's understanding of what drives them and moved them forward. Leaders who possess strong motivation can inspire and motivate others.
4. *Empathy:* the leader's ability to understand others and their needs. An empathetic leader seeks to understand others and appreciate their experiences and views.
5. *Social Skills:* the leader's ability to work with others and get along well with others. A leader who possesses strong social skills can make connections with people from various backgrounds and cultures.

A meta-leader is involved in innovative, forward-thinking practices. One such practice involves the need to attend to effectively manage instructional leadership as a core of a principal's work. Heretofore, instructional leadership was either ignored, not seen within the purview and responsibility of a principal whose primary job was to delegate it to someone else without mindful attention to it (Glanz et al., 2017). The research literature today is replete with an emphasis on the importance of instructional leadership as a core responsibility of a principal.

The framework of instructional leadership presented by Hallinger and Murphy (1985), which is the most widely used in research (Hallinger & Wang, 2015) consists of three dimensions that include ten functions:

- *Defining the school mission*—including two functions: framing the school's goals and communicating the school's goals. Principals are responsible for ensuring a clear mission, which focuses on all students' academic progress, and for disseminating this mission carefully to staff.
- *Managing the instructional program*—including three functions: supervising and evaluating instruction, coordinating curriculum, and monitoring student progress. This dimension focuses on the principals' role in coordinating and controlling the school academic program.
- *Developing a positive school learning climate*—including five functions: protecting instructional time, promoting professional development, maintaining high visibility, providing incentives for teachers, and providing incentives for learning.

Shaked (2021) discusses the imperative of instructional leadership and highlights the following sources. According to Leithwood and Louis (2011), the conceptualization of instructional leadership should include a "set of responsibilities for principals that goes well beyond observing and intervening in classrooms—responsibilities touching on vision, organizational culture and the like" (p. 6). Therefore, they identified four core leadership practices:

- *Setting directions*—defining organizational purposes.
- *Developing people*—expanding the capacities of organizational members to pursue these directions.
- *Redesigning the organization*—modifying the organization to align with and support members' work.
- *Managing instructional program*—improving teaching and curriculum.

A large research base links instructional leadership to positive school outcomes, including improved teacher practices and higher student achievement, in a variety of organizational contexts (e.g., elementary, middle, and high schools; public, private, and public charter), spatial contexts (e.g., urban and suburban schools), and temporal contexts from 1980 through the present (e.g., Glickman et al., 2017). The effect of instructional leadership on student outcomes was found to be three to four times greater than that of transformational leadership, with leaders inspiring, empowering, and stimulating teachers (Supovitz et al., 2010).

A corollary to instructional leadership is the recent attention given to teacher autonomy. Research finds that teacher autonomy is positively associated with teachers' job satisfaction and teacher retention (Worth, 2020). Teachers who perceive that they have less autonomy are more likely to leave their positions, either by moving from one school to another or leaving the profession altogether (Berry et al., 2008). Current literature in the field agrees that teacher autonomy is an important topic for administrators and policy-makers to consider when trying to improve teacher satisfaction and reduce teacher attrition rates.

Teacher empowerment involves investing teachers with the authority to provide input into school goals, curriculum development, and the like. Autonomy is the means by which teachers can take more control over their work. The burgeoning literature on teacher autonomy is significant (Jumani & Malik, 2017). One of the essential lessons in 21st-century schooling is that principals cannot do it alone. They need to empower teachers as professional leaders in their own right. Teacher empowerment through autonomy is aligned with student autonomy as well. Educating in the 21st century calls for a new pedagogy that encourages autonomous learners and shifts the focus from the teacher to the student.

Schleicher (2012) defined four skills as the core of 21st-century learning: Critical thinking, communication, collaboration, and creativity. Others identify six dimensions, collectively referred to as "deeper learning skills" (Martinez and McGrath, 2014), which include the ability to learn how to learn (Huberman et al., 2014). Many other definitions have been suggested (e.g., OECD, 2005), but the common theme of the different definitions is the importance of encouraging autonomous learning and self-motivation. Ultimately, though, it is the role of the principal to model teacher empowerment and foster teacher autonomy (Balvar et al., 2017). Teachers are more likely to empower their students when principals empower teachers (Noi Lee & Nie, 2014).

CLASSIC THEORIES REGARDING AUTONOMY IN THE WORKPLACE

Theory X and Theory Y are two prominent principles of management theory. Frederick Taylor (1911) authored a book titled *The Principles of Scientific Management* in which "efficiency" in managing a school became the watchword of the day. Modeled after a factory, a school and its leaders were expected to efficiently manage school operations according to predetermined criteria or standards. He emphasized that school managers must employ rewards and punishments to motivate employees. The main objective of leadership is to prescribe the correct ways of doing things as perceived by management and then judge their production at the end of the agreed period time.

Douglas McGregor (Kopelman et al., 2008) coined Theory X based on Taylor's hierarchical views of managing schools. Theory X assumes that people dislike work and must be coerced, controlled, and directed toward organizational goals. Teachers are cogs in a machine that can be easily manipulated to suit organizational goals. No effort was made to utilize the employees' experience and knowledge to improve production.

In contrast to Theory X, there is Theory Y in which people can make decisions regarding their behavior beyond self-interests. Work is viewed as a natural inborn trait and workers enjoy a sense of accomplishment and are generally self-motivated.

A significant consequence of Theory Y is that teachers, in our case, possess an innate desire to participate in meaningful professional projects aimed to promote personal growth and student learning. Teachers prefer empowerment and self-autonomy rather than being viewed as "cogs in a machine to be manipulated." Extant research regarding teacher empowerment is premised on the desire of teachers to participate in their professional growth and even in a school's decision-making process.

REVERSE MANAGEMENT IN THE 21ST CENTURY

Reverse management[1] with its origins in the business world, based on Theory Y, is a theory focused on viewing the individual as an initiator rather than a follower of mandates from above in the organization. This concept has relevance for principals who wish to initiate a process of school change by empowering teachers to play an active role in the school. Schools in the 21st century are reconceptualizing the roles of principal and teacher. In other words, reversing, in a sense, the notion that the principal is the chief leader and manager of a school. Rather, shared responsibility for change and improvement is at the core of the educational process in a school.

Another way of looking at it from a reverse management lens is that the principal becomes the manager or architect of the school environment to ensure mechanisms are in place so that teachers can take the lead in a variety of decision-making capacities.

A concept closely aligned with reverse management is the notion of "zooming in" and "zooming out." With teachers more involved in leading instructional improvement efforts by employing strategies such as action research (Altrichter & Posch, 2009), peer coaching (Truesdale, 2009), critical friends (Bambino, 2002), book studies (Sullivan & Glanz, 2013), and, or instructional walk-throughs (City et al., 2010), all which aim to deepen the school's commitment to a culture of instructional excellence, principals can now step back a bit to manage operations from a distance. The role of the principal, thus, becomes a facilitator of change providing resources, material and otherwise, to empower and support teacher autonomy regarding decision-making in areas of curriculum and instruction.

During these times, principals "zoom out" allowing teachers to control aspects of their work in these areas. Parenthetically, by "zooming out," the principal does not abrogate responsibilities as the legal manager-leader of the school. S/he is just empowering teachers to take more active roles in the school. At other times, in contrast, principals do need to "zoom in" to provide situational assistance when necessary, such as managing conflict resolutions, readjusting schedules, and offering suggestions.

Seen in this light, the principles of "adaptive leadership" (Heifetz et al., 2009) come into play to facilitate the change process by encouraging participants of the process to adapt to changing realities. For instance, if teachers are to take control over aspects of their work, school managers need to provide the time resources to allow them to engage in their work with security. The basis of this work is more suited to managing and leading schools in the 21st century, especially when teachers are empowered by assuming greater authority over changes in a school. Hierarchical lines shift. The old paradigms of top-down and bottom-up are dispelled. These conceptions of reimagining leadership and management are not merely a bottom-up design. Rather, as Fullan (2005) has proven, "permeable connectivity" is at play. His research has shown that change that is lasting and meaningful occurs when both top-down (zoom-in) and bottom-up (zoom-out) mechanisms are at play.

The principal in the reverse management realm is removed from the exclusive seat of problem-solving, in favor of a position of more of an observer, listener, and ultimately facilitator of the teachers' proposals. Importantly, it is not that the principal's authority is compromised by the reverse management approach, but rather management and leadership are expressed from a position of mandating and of giving orders, to a position of leading change with a motivated empowered staff.

SUGGESTIONS FOR IMPLEMENTING CHANGE

- Realize that resistance to change is common and should be expected.
- Success is a multi-layered, gradual process that is not always assured, but improvements even though incremental do occur.

- Implement new changes slowly (even one at a time) and provide participants enough time to fully understand expectations and time to build requisite skills to ensure success.
- Give faculty real opportunities to recommend policy changes, e.g., dress codes, mission statement, and curriculum.
- Changing and building a new culture of learning and improvement takes time and continuous commitment. Positive instructional change in any school is inevitably fraught with challenges including resistances and ambivalences. Renewal can occur in time. The school is still in process of developing new ways of learning and improving.
- Schools that have "permeable connectivity" are the most successful in accomplishing meaningful change.
- Principals who provide sufficient support, financial and otherwise, are best at sustaining faculty interest in the specific reform.
- Instructional improvement initiatives should be supported or nested within a larger strategic planning effort (Glanz, 2016).

CONCLUSION

Changing and building a new culture of learning and improvement through empowering teachers certainly takes time and continuous commitment. Schools of the 21st century need leaders who can effectively and efficiently manage the change process. These new breeds of principals realize that leadership and management, as processes and functions, must be well coordinated. Older notions that bifurcate the two processes are no longer relevant in the 21st century.

CASE STUDY

Shazir Mucklai is the recently promoted principal at Kensington High School, with 700 students in grades 9–12. The school has experienced significant changes in demographics over the years, resulting in diverse teacher and student populations. Teachers range quite significantly in age, teaching experience, and years of employment at Kensington. Forty percent of teachers have been in the school from 5–10 years with 25% having been in the school for over 20 years.

However, an influx of new teachers of about 35% (half of whom with 1–5 years of experience, and a half between 11–19 years) coincided with the appointment of Dr. Mucklai. The school has had a traditional top-down hierarchical management structure. Teachers have been generally uninvolved in school operations, and supervision has been conducted by the principal and his assistants with required yearly evaluative observations.

Newly titled Principal Mucklai is forward-thinking about the way a school should function. A progressive, philosophically and educationally, he wants to redefine the school's vision for instructional leadership and supervision. He wants to foster a new vision for leadership and management based on the notion that teachers need to be empowered to become actively engaged in running the school in many ways, including curriculum development and instructional improvement. He knows that introducing this change will surely elicit excitement from some, but resistance from others.

After his first few months of introducing his ideas of teacher empowerment by giving teachers more autonomy, he meets resistance. There is much skepticism among the experienced faculty who have resisted the change process ("reverse management") that Dr. Mucklai introduced. However, a few of the new teachers along with slightly more experienced ones seem receptive, if not enthused. Dr. Mucklai is determined to turn around his school.

Based on ideas culled from this chapter and some of the suggestions offered, as well as your own, what general and specific steps might you take to implement Dr. Mucklai's new vision?

NOTE

1. https://www.odem4u.co.il/index.php?dir=site&page=articles&op=item&cs=3030.

REFERENCES

Altrichter, H., & Posch, P. (2009). Action research, professional development and systemic reform. In S. Noffke & B. Somekh (Eds.), *Educational Action Research* (pp. 231–225). Sage.

Balvar, A., Ozcan, K., & Yildiz, A. (2017). Teacher empowerment: School administrators' roles. *Eurasian Journal of Educational Research, 17*(70), 1–18. http://doi:10.14689/ejer.2017.70.1.

Bambino, D. (2002). Redesigning professional development: Critical friends. *Educational Leadership, 59*(6), 25–27. doi:10.1007/s10459-007-9090-2

Berry, B., Smylie, M., & Fuller, E. (2008). *Understanding teacher working conditions: A review and look to the future.* Center for Teaching Quality. http://www.teachingquality.org/pdfs/ TWC2_Nov08.pdf.

Blasé, J., & Blasé, J. (2004). *Handbook of instructional leadership: How successful principals promote teaching and learning.* Corwin.

Blass, E. (2018). White paper: A 21st-century education paradigm. *Journal of Education & Social Policy 5*(3), 128–133. http://doi.org/10.30845/jesp.v5n3p16.

City, E. A., Elmore, R. F., Fiarman, S. E., & Teitel, L. (2010). *Instructional rounds in education*. Harvard Education Press.

Duffy, F. M. (2016). Organizational arrangements: Supervision and administration—Past and present. In J. Glanz & S. J. Zepeda (Eds.), *Supervision: New perspectives in theory and practice* (pp. 81–96). Rowman & Littlefield.

Fullan, M. (2005). *Leadership and sustainability*. Corwin.

Glanz, J. (2016). Action research by practitioners: A case study of a high school's attempt to create transformational change. *Journal of Practitioner Research, 1*(1), Article 3. http://doi.org/10.5038/2379-9951.1.1.1027. https://scholarcommons.usf.edu/cgi/viewcontent.cgi?referer=&httpsredir=1&article=1027&context=jpr.

Glanz, J., Shaked, H., Rabinowitz, C., Shenhav, S., & Zaretsky, R. (2017). Instructional leadership practices among principals in Israeli and U.S. Jewish Schools. *International Journal of Educational Reform, 26*(2), 132–153. https://drive.google.com/file/d/1TI94pdu9eU95eflyfihEZim6lAw8qotB/view.

Glickman, C. D., Gordon, S. P., & Ross-Gordon, J. M. (2017). *Supervision and instructional leadership: A developmental approach* (9th ed.). Pearson.

Goleman, D., Boyatzis, R., & McKee, A. (2002). *Primal leadership*. Harvard Business School Press.

Hallinger, P., & Heck, R. H. (2011). Exploring the journey of school improvement: Classifying and analyzing patterns of change in school improvement processes and learning outcomes. *School Effectiveness and School Improvement 22*(1), 1–27. https://doi:10.1080/09243453.2010.536322.

Hallinger, P., & Murphy, J. (1985). Assessing the instructional management behavior of principals. *The Elementary School Journal, 86*(2), 217–247. https://doi.org/10.1086/461445.

Hallinger, P., & Wang, W. C. (2015). *Assessing instructional leadership with the principal instructional management rating scale*. Springer.

Heifetz, R. A., Linsky, M., Hallinger, P., & Grashow, A. (2009). *The practice of adaptive leadership: Tools and tactics for changing your organization and the world*. World Harvard Business Press.

Huberman, M., Bitter, C., Anthony, J., & O'Day, J. (2014). *The shape of deeper learning: Strategies, structures, and cultures in deeper learning network high schools*. American Institute for Research. https://files.eric.ed.gov/fulltext/ED553360.pdf.

Jones, K. D., & Ringler, M. C. (2020). Preparing principal candidates to be instructional leaders through virtual coaching preservice teachers. *Journal of Research on Leadership Education, 15*(2), 87–108. https://doi:10.1177/1942775118771379.

Jumani, N. B., & Malik, S. (2017). Promoting teachers' leadership through autonomy and accountability. *Political Science*, 21–41. https://doi:10.1007/978-981-10-4151-8_2.

Kopelman, R., Prottas, D., & Davis, A. (2008). Douglas McGregor's Theory X and Y: Toward a construct-valid measure. *Journal of Managerial Issues, 20*(2), 255–271. http://www.jstor.org/stable/40604607.

Kovacs, H. (2017). Learning and teaching in innovation: Why it is important for education in the 21st Century. *Neveléstudomány Tanulmányok, 2*, 45–60. http://doi.org/10.21549/NTNY.18.2017.2.4.

Leithwood, K., & Louis, K. S. (2011). *Linking leadership to student learning*. John Wiley & Sons.

Marcus, L. J., McNulty, E. J., Henderson, J. M., & Dorn, B. C. (2019). *Crisis, change, and how to lead when it matters most: You're it*. Hachette Book Group.

Martinez, M. R., & McGrath, D. (2014). *Deeper learning: How eight innovative public schools are transforming education in the 21st century*. The New Press.

Morrissey, M. S. (2000). *Professional learning communities: An ongoing exploration*. Southwest Educational Development Library (SEDL).

Noi Lee, A., & Nie, Y. (2014). Understanding teacher empowerment: Teachers' perceptions of principal's and immediate supervisor's empowering behaviours, psychological empowerment and work-related outcomes. *Teaching and Teacher Education, 41*, 67–79. https://doi:10.14689/ejer.2017.70.1.

OECD. (2005). *The definition and selection of key competencies*. OECD. https://www.oecd.org/pisa/35070367.pdf.

Orakcı, S. (Ed.). (2020). *Paradigm shifts in 21st century teaching and learning*. IGI Global. http://doi:10.4018/978-1-7998-3146-4.

Schleicher, A. (Ed.). (2012). *Preparing teachers and developing school leaders for the 21st century: Lessons from around the world*. OECD Publishing. https://www.oecd.org/site/eduistp2012/49850576.pdf.

Shaked, H. (2019). School leaders' contribution to social justice. *International Journal of Educational Reform, 28*(3), 303–316. https://doi:10.1177/1056787919857259.

Shaked, H. (2021). Instructional leadership in times of crises and the goal of schooling. In J. Glanz, (Ed.), *Crisis and pandemic leadership: Implications for principals, teachers, and parents*. Rowman & Littlefield.

Shenhav S, Geffon A, Salomon L, & Glanz J. (2020). Encouraging and discouraging factors in the decision to become an Israeli leader in religious schools: Implications for reforming bureaucratic mandates of the ministry of education. *International Journal of Educational Reform, 30*(1), 77–97. https://doi:10.1177/1056787920957029.

Stark, M. D., McGhee, M. W., & Jimerson, J. B. (2017). Reclaiming instructional Supervision: Using solution-focused strategies to promote teacher development. *Journal of Research on Leadership Education, 12*(3), 215–238. https://doi:10.1177/1942775116684895.

Stronge, J. H. (2007). *Qualities of effective teaching* (2nd ed.). Association for Supervision and Curriculum Development.

Sullivan, S., & Glanz, J. (2006). *Building effective learning communities: Strategies for leadership, learning, and collaboration*. Corwin.

Sullivan, S., & Glanz, J. (2013). *Supervision that improves teaching and learning: Strategies and techniques* (4th ed.). Corwin.

Supovitz, J., Sirinides, P., & May, H. (2010). How principals and peers influence teaching and learning. *Educational Administration Quarterly, 46*(1), 31–56. https://doi.org/10.1177/1094670509353043.

Taylor, F. W. (1911). *The principles of scientific management*. Harper & Brothers.
Truesdale, W. (2009). *Peer coaching on transferability of staff development*. Lambert Academic Publishing.
Worth, J. (2020). How does autonomy relate to job satisfaction and retention in teaching? https://impact.chartered.college/article/how-does-autonomy-job-satisfaction-retention-teaching/.

Chapter Three

Supporting Technology Integration in Schools

In Pursuit of New Skills for School Managers in the Post-Pandemic Era

Köksal Banoğlu & Sedat Gümüş

INTRODUCTION

With the rapid penetration of information and communication technology (ICT) into schools in the early 1990s, a rhetorical question of whether educational technologies would replace teachers in classrooms had then provided a great deal of intellectual stimulation for educational practitioners around the globe (Light, 2001; Tyack & Cuban, 1995; Oblinger & Oblinger, 2005; Oppenheimer, 2003). This sort of hypothetical thinking had also quickly polarized educational scholars into two camps (Cuban, 2001).

On the one hand, advocates of technological determinism expected schools to be thoroughly digitized by expanding their virtual fabrics in newly emerging human-human (e.g., social media), human-object (e.g., robotic teachers), and object-object (e.g., e-document systems) interactions beyond school walls (Kanda et al., 2004; VanLehn, 2011). From this techno-centric viewpoint, it was obvious that ICT devices would quickly mold school communities to fit their pattern in every sense (Houser, 2017; Seldon & Abidoye, 2018).

On the other hand, those who espouse a kind of social determinism gave credence to societal and economic systems in which technology users are embedded, but not to the technology itself (Pflaum, 2004; Watson, 2010). They acclaimed ICT as a strategic medium for its efficiency to facilitate organizational goals in service of its hopefully qualified users (Cuban, 2001).

In the wake of the COVID-19 pandemic, however, this long-debated dichotomy has fallen off the education agenda (Breines & Gallagher, 2020). Teachers are playing a pivotal role in distance learning because education has gone through an accelerated digital transformation (Delcker & Ifenthaler, 2020). It seems that the so-called *"human versus machine"* antagonism has receded into science-fiction narratives (Bayne, 2015). Instead, it is now much more discussed in academic and policymaker circles how "human and machine" have to work together to deliver digital educational solutions in all facets of life (Moursund, 2015; Sims-Bainbridge, 2008). In schools, particularly, technology had already become a crucial component of teaching and learning as well as the management processes even before the pandemic era in many countries. The recent developments related to the pandemic strengthened this trend and made technology an indispensable part of the educational activities, both within and beyond the school walls.

In this chapter, we set out to compile the role of technology in the day-to-day practices of school managers based on the existing international literature. To that end, we first provide a historical overview of the ICT integration into K-12 school systems. Among miscellaneous ICT integration models, we draw on the most-known two models: (1) technology acceptance model (TAM; Davis, 1989) and (2) technological pedagogical content knowledge model (TPACK; Mishra & Koehler, 2006). We introduce these models concerning the opportunities and challenges they have brought into the complex work of the school management. As such, we open up a discussion about the effect of the COVID-19 pandemic and resulting post-pandemic remote-school implementations on school management in light of the introduced ICT integration models. Lastly, we provide a list of suggestions for school managers' ICT use in their daily management practices as well as for their efforts to promote ICT integration in their schools.

EDUCATIONAL TECHNOLOGIES AND INTEGRATION MODELS

The definition of educational technologies extends far beyond a list of artifacts and devices, involving processes, applied knowledge, and methods that facilitate teaching and learning as a whole (Friesen, 2013). Through the invention of writing and reading technologies, for instance, clay tablets, parchment, paper, and printing, literate people had larger access to information by adopting these technologies in their "free time" (Gr. scholè, Fr. école). Without this initial alphabetical technologization of the wor(l)d, it is clear that education and school could not transmit the wisdom of previous generations to new ones in the form of culture (Masschelein, 2011).

On the flip side, almost two-and-a-half millennia ago, probably the first criticism of these educational technologies was given by Plato who, speaking through Socrates in the Phaedrus, denounced the use of "writing" as a challenge to the dialogic relationship between teacher and student (Schiff, 2020). His major concern was that technological mediums might determine the quality of our pedagogical interactions (Feenberg, 2001). Hence, the clarity of nonverbal communication is dependent upon the mechanic order of written letters and words that are fixed, once and for all, in the corpus of educational texts (Vlieghe, 2014). Plato's critical stance against the static embodiment of knowledge in written texts was again echoed in the educational debates of the second half of the 20th century over whether educational technologies reflect neutral mediums of learning as external assets or reflexive processes that require compresence and social interaction of teacher and students (Hamilton, 2016).

The fast and pervasive diffusion of digitized technologies into daily life in the 1990s seemed to render that ill-communication argument invalid to a large extent (Bruce, 1996). ICT integration research, therefore, shifted the focus from technical capacity of medium-objects to human-subjects, such as teachers and students' individual features (e.g., beliefs, attitudes, readiness) and barriers (e.g., anxiety, fears, access) to ICT deployment in education (Davis, 1989, 1993; Mishra & Koehler, 2006; Ertmer, 1999; Mumtaz, 2000). Since then, digital streams have been much further developed in facilitating real-time communication and reciprocal exchange both verbally and nonverbally. By extension, the social aspect of educational technologies had made teacher-student dialogues more highly interactive within and beyond school walls (Kim & Lee, 2020). In the following section, we introduce two ICT integration models mentioned above and argue those models for their theoretical and practical implications in relation to today's (post)pandemic school management practices.

Technology Acceptance Model (TAM)

Both perceptual facilitators and obstacles to users' technology acceptance have long been debated in management scholarship. When dating back to 1985, the first version of TAM provided a sound theoretical ground to explain why and how technology users come to accept ICT in their daily practices (Davis, 1989). The driving assumption behind the TAM is that internalization of technology usage results from users' subjective perception of easiness in adopting the target technology. This linkage is mediated by the relationship between what attitude the users hold toward the target technology and how useful they perceive that technology in practice. The underlying causal order of this early model (i.e., perceived easiness > usefulness and attitude > actual use) also motivated some scholars to replicate and extend it to the TAM-2 (Venkatesh & Davis, 2000) and TAM-3 (Venkatesh & Bala, 2008). In these extended models, a long list of potential facilitators and some obstacles were additionally involved, such as users' demographics, voluntariness, experience, and so on.

Research conducted in educational settings has also benefitted greatly from TAM (Nair & Das, 2011; Teo, 2009; Totolo, 2011; Yuen & Ma, 2008). Such research is primarily interested in determining the factors affecting teachers' acceptance of technology. Along with other personal and external factors, school management also emerged as an important factor affecting teachers' acceptance (Demetriadis et al., 2003; Huang & Teo, 2020; Polizzi, 2011). Research has revealed that managers' technology competence and attitudes, their efforts to create a positive culture toward technology, and professional development opportunities they provided to teachers might be catalyzers for teachers' acceptance as well as actual technology use (Afshari et al., 2008; Huang & Teo, 2020; Polizzi, 2011).

In the present chapter, we bring up the discussion that after the pandemic TAMs may need further revisions in some aspects. First, because of the advent of online learning management systems (LMSs) and their rapid incorporation to K–12 schools by remote-school implementations, teachers' use of ICT shifted from being an option to be an obligation. When considering this shift, we propose that teachers' acceptance of technology is no longer the issue in terms of their willingness to use ICT. However, we also note that the compulsory digitalization process brings a heavy burden on teachers and school managers' shoulders, as part of that so-called "new normal" job context. Therefore, it may become a new obstacle against the quality of ICT use in education, which has surprisingly never been issued in the TAMs.

With the new dynamics brought by the pandemic and rapid technology integration, we believe that the role of school managers has become even more crucial, specifically for the betterment of teachers' and students' ICT experiences. Challenge is no longer convincing teachers to use ICT in teaching, but ensuring that they are equipped with the best resources and receive technical as well as emotional support. First, and more obviously, school managers affect the process by providing up-to-date and functional infrastructure as well as appropriate technical support (Mirzajani et al., 2016; Tołwińska, 2021, Wang, 2010). School managers' active encouragement, motivation, and support can also make a substantial difference in the quality of teachers' ICT use.

It is now even more important for school managers to be competent technology users and act as role models by effectively integrating ICT in their daily practices, especially when working/communicating with teachers. In addition, providing teachers with the best LMS, ICT devices, and online learning tools, employing enough and competent support staff for ICT integration, and communicating regularly with teachers to hear their ICT-related challenges are now among the most important roles of school managers. Given the specific remote teaching implementations in the pandemic era, offering emotional support and comfort to teachers, students, and parents through their individual knowledge and experiences have also become an important skill for school managers to make sure the effective implementation of virtual learning.

Technology Pedagogical Content Knowledge (TPACK) Model

The TPACK model emphasizes the content area of taught lessons in relation to technological and pedagogical knowledge fields (Mishra & Koehler, 2006). The heart of this model is that a teacher's pedagogical content knowledge (PCK) harnesses the power of ICT as an accelerator so that a teacher can adopt ICT-related content knowledge (TCK) for getting course materials and content into line with their techno-pedagogical knowledge (TPK). In the simplest terms, those who utilize the TPACK model advocate that effective teaching practice is closely interwoven with teacher's knowledge fields of student learning (i.e., pedagogy), knowledge of the subject field (i.e., content), and mastery of instructional tools (i.e., technology) in practice (Koehler, Mishra & Cain, 2013).

The TPACK model emphasizes the role of teachers' knowledge in different components of teaching with ICT. In this model, therefore, developing teachers' knowledge gains great importance for the success of ICT integration (Bos, 2011; Kafyulilo et al., 2016; Koh et al., 2018). As mentioned in the relevant literature, school managers play a substantial role in this process. School managers' influence mostly stems from the learning opportunities they provide to teachers either through their daily interactions (e.g., communications and feedback on technology use) and/or structured professional development opportunities (e.g., training programs, collaborative practices).

Research has shown that teachers integrate technology into their practice more when they receive adequate time and resources for training (Hsu & Kuan, 2013; Peled et al., 2011). Thus, school managers' effort to allocate more time and resources for training on ICT integration can improve teachers' techno-pedagogical knowledge and ease the process of linking it to their content knowledge. Given the steady increase in the use of ICT for teachers' professional development over the years as well as the rapid changes brought by the COVID-19 pandemic, we believe that such professional development activities can also benefit significantly from online tools (Dede et al., 2009; Philipsen et al., 2019; Sheridan et al., 2020).

First, school managers can plan and offer seminars/workshops by using video conferencing tools (e.g., Zoom, Google Meet, and Microsoft Teams) that teachers around the world now use frequently in their daily practice (Maher & Prescott, 2017; Safi et al., 2020). Those who manage the technological program should encourage and reward teachers' self-directed online learning efforts, such as attending Massive Open Online Courses (MOOCs) or using professional development websites (Beach, 2017; Castaño-Muñoz et al., 2018; Misra, 2018).

Research on teacher professional learning has also illustrated that despite being important PD activities in the forms of seminars or workshops do not always bring changes in teachers' instructional practices (Hill et al., 2013). Rather, collaboration among colleagues and networking activities have a higher potential to make difference in practice (Althauser, 2015; Banoğlu, 2019; Gümüş & Bellibaş, 2021). Therefore, providing teachers with opportunities to collaborate in terms of the application of ICT tools and methods seems to be crucial for transferring the acquired knowledge into practice and making sure of continuous improvement (Tołwińska, 2021; Tondeur et al., 2016). School managers can do this in various ways such as requiring collaborative online discussions, planning structured virtual group activities, encouraging knowledge and experience sharing on the internet, and so on.

PRACTICAL SUGGESTIONS FOR DAILY PRACTICES OF SCHOOL MANAGERS

Lastly, we would like to provide a list of suggestions for school managers regarding their ICT use in daily managerial practices as well as their efforts to promote ICT integration in teaching and learning activities in their schools. We based our suggestions on several studies from different contexts (Attaran & VanLaar, 2001; Afshari et al., 2009; Tołwińska, 2021; Yee, 2000).

- Focus on your ICT competence and be a role model for continuous learning and development.
- Get help from experts when you need it and participate in peer networks.
- Integrate ICT in your daily administrative practices, such as keeping records, data storage and analysis, budgeting, reporting, and communication.
- Model effective use of technological devices and online tools when communicating with stakeholders (e.g., students, teachers, parents).
- Create a vision and strategies for ICT integration in the teaching and learning process in collaboration with teachers, ICT specialists and other staff.
- Provide the best possible equipment, LMS, and technical support aligning with the developed vision and strategies.
- Ease teachers', students', and other stakeholders' access to ICT devices not only in classrooms but also in hallways, computer labs, etc.
- Monitor and administer the integration of ICT in teaching activities through formal and informal interactions with teachers and students.

- Provide opportunities and encouragement for teachers' professional development on ICT.
- Integrate various ICT devices and online tools into the planned PD activities.
- Acknowledge and reward the best practices as well as collaboration and knowledge sharing among teachers.
- Be open-minded and encourage creativity and innovation among teachers and students regarding the use of ICT.
- Be supportive, try to increase motivation for ICT integration, and reduce the related anxiety and stress.
- Be aware of ethical and legal issues related to ICT use and communicate those with all relevant stakeholders.

CONCLUSION

It is not clear for now how long the post-pandemic period of remote-school implementations will last. Nonetheless, there is more than enough reason to assume that this period will have some persistent effect on traditional in-person education from now on. School principals are to take on a more proactive role in providing teachers with the best resources as well as offering them technical and emotional supports in the post-pandemic era. Role modeling in terms of daily practices of ICT usage and supporting the professional development of teachers in various ways, as explained above, will be more crucial for successful ICT implementations. School principals' participation in professional learning networks with their staff is particularly important to promote teacher well-being and teacher learning through their engagement in online interactions.

To better exemplify our points to readers, we present the following case study including an average high school from the pre-pandemic era. It is centered on a school principal's immediate confusion about the remote-school implementation when the pandemic kicked in. The case includes situations that you might have encountered in your school/work experience and provides some questions to consider for future improvements.

CASE STUDY

Teachers at Wellington High School have always felt well-supported and respected by Mrs. Betty Whittier, a ten-year tenured principal in her sixties. As a beloved school manager who has built her career on empowering teachers to take an active role in instructional practices and their learning process, Mrs. Whittier allows her colleagues to make personal choices about whether or not to use ICT tools in the classroom. She strongly believes that people only take action on what they perceive to be critical to the achievement of their objectives; otherwise, they just go through the motions.

Due to Mrs. Whittier's libertarian management perspective, there was a feeling of release and freedom in the air throughout the school. Suddenly, however, everything changed, and the changes came fast when the outbreak of the COVID-19 pandemic brought about successive lockdowns, curfews, and school closures across the country. This has become a true game-changer for Mrs. Whittier and all teachers in terms of how they were confronted with the newly emerging challenges of digitalized classrooms and the remote-school experience after the pandemic.

During the first online faculty meeting, it was clear on their faces all board members were caught off guard by the district's decision of online education. Teachers remained frozen looking at the screen in silence for a while when they were asked whether they had ever experienced synchronous virtual classrooms and prepared asynchronous teaching materials by online presentation software. A middle-aged teacher raised his hand and replied with a self-assured tone: "Yes, I had experience at my previous school because our school principal had invested in a learning management system to streamline online material and resource sharing." Other teachers were not as confident. Frustration and, even, fear were predominant. Teachers silently wondered if they were indeed able to weather this unexpected storm on their own.

If you were in the shoes of Mrs.Whittier, which technology leadership and management behaviors should you have exercised long before the storm began? How would you face the oncoming storm and a possible mutiny on the way? Please motivate your answer with some theoretical and practical ideas from this chapter.

REFERENCES

Afshari, M., Bakar, K. A., Luan, W. S., Samah, B. A., & Fooi, F. S. (2008). School leadership and information communication technology. *Turkish Online Journal of Educational Technology-TOJET*, 7(4), 82–91.

Afshari, M., Bakar, K. A., Luan, W. S., Samah, B. A., & Fooi, F. S. (2009). Technology and school leadership. *Technology, Pedagogy and Education,* 18(2), 235–248. https://doi.org/10.1080/14759390902992527

Althauser, K. (2015). Job-embedded professional development: Its impact on teacher self-efficacy and student performance. *Teacher Development,* 19(2), 210–225. https://doi.org/10.1080/13664530.2015.1011346

Attaran, M., & VanLaar, I. (2001). Managing the use of school technology: An eight step guide for administrators. *Journal of Management Development, 20*(5), 393–401. https://doi.org/10.1108/02621710110421697.

Banoğlu, K. (2019). *Multivariate analysis of school principals' technology leadership competencies, learning school environment and schools' social network structures.* Unpublished PhD Thesis. Ghent University, Faculty of Psychology and Educational Sciences; Marmara Üniversitesi, EğitimBilimleriEnstitüsü. Ghent, Belgium; Istanbul, Turkey.

Bayne, S. (2015). Teacherbot: Interventions in automated teaching. *Teaching in Higher Education, 20*(4), 455–467. https://doi.org/10.1080/13562517.2015.1020783.

Beach, P. (2017). Self-directed online learning: A theoretical model for understanding elementary teachers' online learning experiences. *Teaching and Teacher Education, 61*, 60–72. https://doi.org/10.1016/j.tate.2016.10.007.

Bos, B. (2011). Professional development for elementary teachers using TPACK. *Contemporary Issues in Technology and Teacher Education, 11*(2). https://citejournal.org/volume-11/issue-2-11/mathematics/professional-development-for-elementary-teachers-using-tpack.

Breines, M. R., & Gallagher, M. (2020). A return to teacherbot: Rethinking the development of educational technology at the University of Edinburgh. *Teaching in Higher Education.* Advance online publication. https://doi.org/10.1080/13562517.2020.1825373.

Bruce, B. C. (1996). Technology as social practice. *Educational Foundations. 10*(4), 51–58.

Castaño-Muñoz, J., Kalz, M., Kreijns, K., & Punie, Y. (2018). Who is taking MOOCs for teachers' professional development on the use of ICT? A cross-sectional study from Spain. *Technology, Pedagogy and Education, 27*(5), 607–624. http://dx.doi.org/10.1080/1475939X.2018.1528997.

Cuban, L. (2001). *Oversold and underused: Computers in the classroom.* Harvard University Press.

Davis, F. D. (1989). Perceived usefulness, perceived ease of use, and user acceptance of information technology. *MIS Quarterly, 19*(2), 319–340. https://doi.org/10.2307/249008.

Davis, F. D. (1993). User acceptance of information technology: System characteristics, user perceptions and behavioral impacts. *International Journal of Man-Machine Studies, 38*(3), 475–487. https://doi.org/10.1006/imms.1993.1022.

Dede, C., JassKetelhut, D., Whitehouse, P., Breit, L., & McCloskey, E. M. (2009). A research agenda for online teacher professional development. *Journal of Teacher Education, 60*(1), 8–19. https://doi.org/10.1177/0022487108327554.

Delcker, J., & Ifenthaler, D. (2020). Teachers' perspective on school development at German vocational schools during the COVID-19 pandemic. *Technology, Pedagogy and Education.* Advance online publication. https://doi.org/10.1080/1475939X.2020.1857826.

Demetriadis, S., Barbas, A., Molohides, A., Palaigeorgiou, G., Psillos, D., Vlahavas, I., & Pombortsis, A. (2003). "Cultures in negotiation": Teachers' acceptance/resistance attitudes considering the infusion of technology into schools. *Computers & Education, 41*(1), 19–37. https://doi.org/10.1016/S0360-1315(03)00012-5.

Ertmer, P. A. (1999). Addressing first-and second-order barriers to change: Strategies for technology integration. *Educational Technology Research and Development, 47*(4), 47–61. https://doi.org/10.1007/BF02299597.

Feenberg, A. (2001). Whither educational technologies? *International Journal of Technology and Design Education, 11,* 83–91. https://doi.org/10.1023/A:1011225903766.

Friesen, N. (2013). Educational technology and the 'new Language of Learning': lineage and limitations. In N. Selwyn & K. Facer (Eds.), *The politics of education and technology: Conflicts, controversies and connections* (pp. 21–38). Palgrave.

Gümüş, E., & Bellibaş, M. Ş. (2021). The relationship between the types of professional development activities teachers participate in and their self-efficacy: A multi-country analysis. *European Journal of Teacher Education.* Online First. https://doi.org/10.1080/02619768.2021.1892639.

Hamilton, E. C. (2016). The age of automation: The technical code of online education to 1980. In E. C. Hamilton (Ed.), *Technology and the politics of university reform. The social shaping of online education. Palgrave Macmillan's digital education and learning* (pp. 47–72). Palgrave Macmillan. https://doi.org/10.1057/9781137503510_3.

Hill, H. C., Beisiegel, M., & Jacob, R. (2013). Professional development research: Consensus, crossroads, and challenges. *Educational Researcher, 42*(9), 476–487. https://doi.org/10.3102/0013189X13512674.

Houser, K. (2017, December 11). The solution to our education crisis might be AI. *Futurism.* https://futurism.com/ai-teachers-education-crisis.

Hsu, S., & Kuan, P. Y. (2013). The impact of multilevel factors on technology integration: The case of Taiwanese grade 1–9 teachers and schools. *Educational Technology Research and Development, 61,* 25–50. https://doi.org/10.1007/s11423-012-9269-y.

Huang, F., & Teo, T. (2020). Influence of teacher-perceived organisational culture and school policy on Chinese teachers' intention to use technology: An extension of technology acceptance model. *Educational Technology Research & Development, 68,* 1547–1567. https://doi.org/10.1007/s11423-019-09722-y.

Kafyulilo, A., Fisser, P., & Voogt, J. (2016). Factors affecting teachers' continuation of technology use in teaching. *Education and Information Technologies, 21,* 1535–1554. https://doi.org/10.1007/s10639-015-9398-0.

Kanda, T., Hirano, T., Eaton, D., & Ishiguro, H. (2004). Interactive robots as social partners and peer tutors for children: A field trial. *Human-Computer Interaction, 19,* 61–84.

Kim, Y., & Lee D. Y. (2020). 3D Hologram learning kit development for elementary education. In P. Zaphiris & A. Ioannou (Eds.), *Learning and collaboration technologies. Human and technology ecosystems. HCII 2020* (pp. 464–479). Springer, Cham. https://doi.org/10.1007/978-3-030-50506-6_32.

Koehler, M. J., Mishra, P., & Cain, W. (2013). What is technological pedagogical content knowledge (TPACK)? *Journal of Education, 193*(3), 13–20. https://doi.org/10.1177/002205741319300303.

Koh, J. H. L., Chai, C. S., & Lim, W. Y. (2017). Teacher professional development for TPACK-21CL: Effects on teacher ICT integration and student outcomes. *Journal of Educational Computing Research, 55*(2), 172–196. https://doi.org/10.1177/0735633116656848.

Light, J. (2001). Rethinking the digital divide. *Harvard Educational Review, 71*(4), 709–733. https://doi.org/10.17763/haer.71.4.342x36742j2w4q82.

Maher, D., & Prescott, A. (2017). Professional development for rural and remote teachers using video conferencing. *Asia-Pacific Journal of Teacher Education, 45*(5), 520–538. https://doi.org/10.1080/1359866X.2017.1296930\.

Masschelein, J. (2011). Experimentum scholae: The world once more. . . . But not (yet) finished. *Studies in Philosophy and Education, 30*(5), 529–535. https://doi.org/10.1007/s11217-011-9257-4.

Mirzajani, H., Mahmud, R., Ayub, A. F. M., & Wong, S. L. (2016). Teachers' acceptance of ICT and its integration in the classroom. *Quality Assurance in Education, 24*(1), 26–40.https://doi.org/10.1108/QAE-06-2014-0025.

Mishra, P., & Koehler, M. J. (2006). Technological pedagogical content knowledge: A framework for teacher knowledge. *Teachers College Record, 108*(6), 1017–1054. https://doi.org/10.1111/j.1467-9620.2006.00684.x.

Misra, P. K. (2018). MOOCs for teacher professional development: Reflections and suggested actions. *Open Praxis, 10*(1), 67–77. http://dx.doi.org/10.5944/openpraxis.10.1.780.

Moursund, D. (2015). The first machine age. In D. Moursund & Robert Sylwester (Eds.), *Education for Students' Future* (pp. 12–17). Information Age Education. https://i-a-e.org/downloads/free-ebooks-by-dave-moursund/269-education-for-students-futures-1/file.html.

Mumtaz, S. (2000). Factors affecting teachers' use of information and communications technology: A review of the literature. *Technology, Pedagogy and Education, 9*, 319–342. https://doi.org/10.1080/14759390000200096.

Nair, I., & Das, V. M. (2011). Analysis of recent studies undertaken for assessing acceptance of technology among teachers using TAM. *International Journal of Computer Applications, 32*(8), 38–46.

Oblinger, D. G., & Oblinger, J. L. (2005). *Educating the next generation.* Educase. https://www.educause.edu/ir/library/PDF/pub7101.pdf.

Oppenheimer, T. (2003). *The flickering mind: The false promise of technology in the classroom and how learning can be saved.* Random House.

Peled, Y., Kali, Y., & Dori, Y. J. (2011). School principals' influence on science teachers' technology implementation: A retrospective analysis. *International Journal of leadership in Education, 14*(2), 229–245. https://doi.org/10.1080/13603124.2010.524249.

Pflaum, W. D. (2004). *The technology fix.* Association for Supervision and Curriculum Development.

Philipsen, B., Tondeur, J., Roblin, N. P., Vanslambrouck, S., & Zhu, C. (2019). Improving teacher professional development for online and blended learning: A systematic meta-aggregative review. *Educational Technology Research and Development, 67*(5), 1145–1174. https://doi.org/10.1007/s11423-019-09645-8.

Polizzi, G. (2011). Measuring school principals' support for ICT integration in Palermo, Italy. *Journal of Media Literacy Education*, *3*(2), 113–122.

Safi, F., Wenzel, T., & Spalding, L. A. T. (2020). Remote learning community: Supporting teacher educators during unprecedented times. *Journal of Technology and Teacher Education*, *28*(2), 211–222.

Scanga, L. H., Deen, M. Y., Smith, S. R., & Wright, K. (2018). Zoom around the world: Using videoconferencing technology for international trainings. *Journal of Extension*, *56*(5). https://tigerprints.clemson.edu/joe/vol56/iss5/14.

Schiff, D. (2020). Out of the laboratory and into classroom: The future of artificial intelligence in education. *Artificial Intelligence & Society*, *36*, 331–348. https://doi.org/10.1007/s00146-020-01033-8.

Seldon, A., & Abidoye, O. (2018). *The fourth education revolution*. Buckingham University Press.

Sheridan, K. M., Banzer, D., Pradzinski, A., & Wen, X. (2020). Early math professional development: Meeting the challenge through online learning. *Early Childhood Education Journal*, *48*(2), 223–231. https://doi.org/10.1007/s10643-019-00992-y.

Sims-Bainbridge, W. (2008). The convergence of sociology and computer science. In H. Hartman (Ed.), *Integrating the sciences and society: Challenges, practices, and potentials* (pp. 257–275). Emerald Group Publishing.

Teo, T. (2009). The impact of subjective norm and facilitating conditions on pre-service teachers' attitude toward computer use: A structural equation modeling of an extended technology acceptance model. *Journal of Educational Computing Research*, *40*(1), 89–109. https://doi.org/10.2190/EC.40.1.d.

Tołwińska, B. (2021). The role of principals in learning schools to support teachers' use of digital technologies. *Technology, Knowledge and Learning*, 1–14. https://doi.org/10.1007/s10758-021-09496-4.

Tondeur, J., Forkosh-Baruch, A., Prestridge, S., Albion, P., & Edirisinghe, S. (2016). Responding to challenges in teacher professional development for ICT integration in education. *Educational Technology and Society*, *19*(3), 110–120.

Totolo, A. (2011). Adoption and use of computer technology among school principals in Botswana secondary schools. *The International Information & Library Review*, *43*(2), 70–78. https://doi.org/10.1080/10572317.2011.10762882.

Tyack, D., & Cuban, L. (1995). *Tinkering toward utopia. A century of public school reform*. Harvard University Press.

VanLehn, K. (2011). The relative effectiveness of human tutoring, intelligent tutoring systems, and other tutoring systems. *Educational Psychologist*, *46*(4), 197–221. https://doi.org/10.1080/00461520.2011.611369.

Venkatesh, V., & Bala, H. (2008). Technology acceptance model 3 and a research agenda on interventions. *Decision Science*, *39*(2), 273–312. https://doi.org/10.1111/j.1540-5915.2008.00192.x.

Venkatesh, V., & Davis, F.D. (2000). A theoretical extension of the technology acceptance model: Four longitudinal field studies. *Management Science*, *46*(2), 186–204.

Vlieghe, J. (2014). Education in an age of digital technologies Flusser, Stiegler, and Agamben on the idea of the posthistorical. *Philosophy and Technology, 27*(4), 519–537.https://doi.org/10.1007/s13347-013-0131-x.

Wang, C. H. (2010). Technology leadership among school principals: A technology-coordinator's perspective. *Asian Social Science, 6*(1), 51. https://doi.org/10.5539/ass.v6n1p51.

Watson, R. (2010). *Future minds. How the digital age is changing our minds, why this matters, and what we can do about it*. Nicholas Brealey Publishing.

Yee, D. L. (2000). Images of school principals' information and communications technology leadership. *Journal of Information Technology for Teacher Education, 9*(3), 287–302. https://doi.org/10.1080/14759390000200097.

Yuen, A. H., & Ma, W. W. (2008). Exploring teacher acceptance of e-learning technology. *Asia-Pacific Journal of Teacher Education, 36*(3), 229–243. https://doi.org/10.1080/13598660802232779.

Chapter Four

Basic Principles of Teacher Evaluation Examined for School Leaders in the 21st Century

Helen M. Hazi

INTRODUCTION[1]

Managing today's schools is more complicated than ever. Promoting teacher quality, via teacher evaluation, remains high on every school's agenda. This focus in the United States in the name of accountability has weighed heavily for the past two decades on educators. If the public funds schools with their tax dollars, the public has a right and responsibility to ask how its money promotes high standards, quality, and equity in the schools. However, educators, in the 21st century, should acknowledge dysfunction, when accountability plans become extreme, high-stakes, or result in harmful consequences to students or employees.

My colleague Ed Pajak (2011) critically examined educational reform efforts by arguing that these recipes for improving education represent a "narcissistic education policy style . . . [that] denies the true learning needs of students, . . . disempowers classroom teachers . . . and reproduces narcissistic dynamics within our culture" (pp. 2019–2020). Using a socio-cultural lens and citing Lasch's (1978) work on cultural narcissism, Pajak maintained that the same theme dominates initiatives that produce a preoccupation with control and alignment, an obsession with tests and objectives, and overconfidence in technological solutions.

Even with a reprieve from using student test scores to evaluate teachers by the *Every Student Succeeds Act* (2015), few states took advantage of it, due to investments made in time, professional development, and instruments with online platforms linked to convenient three-minute videos for teachers (Hazi, 2014; Leahy, 2012). Locked in two decades of use, both teachers and leaders seem to cling to teacher evaluation's promise to improve instruction, despite the many barriers and the few studies where evaluation has done so (Donaldson, 2021; Reinhorn et al., 2017). Even during the COVID-19 pandemic, as U.S. leaders and policymakers alike were torn between online or in-person instruction, administrators are bargaining with teacher unions about how evaluation had to occur in the strained environment of hybrid teaching and learning (Hemphill & Marianno, 2021).

It is within this complex socio-cultural context, that I asked and continue to ask educators to return to their roots, rather than to immediately jump to develop a new rubric to evaluate online teaching (Schaffhauser, 2020; Williams, 2020) though they may be tempted to do so. Teacher evaluation has become a complex public-school practice influenced by many disciplines (e.g., law and psychology) and many discourses (e.g., administration, supervision, and psychometrics).

However, some argue that evaluation is a discipline unto itself (Scriven, 1994). This author returns to her roots in the discipline of evaluation to examine its foundation for teacher evaluation, the annual practice of rating teachers to make personnel decisions.[2] The purpose of this chapter is to offer principles for teacher evaluation that are relevant for a changing educational environment in the 21st century. In the first section, I draw on the definitions and principles from the discourse community of evaluation represented by scholars such as Michael Scriven and Daniel Stufflebeam. In the second section, I offer principles to guide educator action. The chapter concludes with a summary and case studies.

PRINCIPLES FOR UNDERSTANDING EVALUATION

The principles in this section address evaluation of the individual teacher. They include the (mis)use of formative and summative; the importance of distancing; the role of self-evaluation; the importance of goal-free, but needs based evaluation; the value of evaluating both generic and particular duties; restoring multiple methods and sources of evidence; and the misplaced focus on accuracy over utility.

Although this section addresses current practice, teacher evaluation in the 21st century and beyond could very well occur in groups as school improvement evolves under the aegis of Improvement Science (Bryk, 2015; LeMahieu et al., 2017), an emerging discourse recognizing the complexity of improvement in schools and higher education institutions. Key concepts of Improvement Science include systems thinking, networked improvement communities, and expecting variation rather than standardization of processes and outcomes.

For example, networks of teachers may use lesson study to improve their teaching (Hiebert & Stigler, 2017). Teacher discussions could occur in the same grade level across schools, or in the same subject across districts, in similar specialties such as special education across states, or any imaginable combination. These networks may constitute "safe space" where teachers disclose information that will help them set goals for experimentation that leads to improvement. Leaders may encourage teachers to use evidence from those networks for their evaluation. At the end of this chapter, you will be asked to imagine these possibilities; but for now, think about the evaluation of individual teachers.

The formative and summative. The terms "formative" and "summative" came to be used during the 1960s when schools began receiving funds to evaluate federal education programs (Popham, 2013). In an influential essay, Michael Scriven (1967) distinguished between the two. The purpose of formative evaluation was to determine the worth of a new education program to improve it, while the purpose of summative evaluation was to determine the worth of a completed program to help decide its continuation or termination. The two then were applied to personnel evaluation. Formative evaluation was used to provide feedback to improve during the year, while summative evaluation was done at the end of the year to provide a final rating to inform personnel decisions such as termination, tenure, and rewards.

Many educators and scholars believe that both formative and summative evaluation can be vested in the same system and in the same person (e.g., Hunter, 1988). Some have argued that the purposes are contradictory (e.g., Popham, 1988; Kraft et al., 2018) and systems that develop and measure look very different (Marzano, 2012). Most administrators believe that they can be vested in the same individual where there is time, trust, and training (e.g., Hunter, 1988). Teachers tend to see these purposes as incompatible and irreconcilable in the same person (Hazi, 1994) and find improvement information useful when it comes from those in the same content area (Hazi, 2021). However, Scriven (1996) sees them as very different functions that were never meant to be performed by the same individual, the principal.

Distancing. With the difficulty of combining formative and summative in one role, Scriven (1996) believes that evaluators should be distanced from those they evaluate. Distancing helps the evaluator maintain objectivity, be free of any conflict of interest, and avoid compromising its validity. Distance also allows "the evaluand," the one evaluated, to implement the recommendations offered. Scriven suggests that we think of a continuum where objectivity and ownership of evaluation's results are at one end and teacher rejection of results and evaluator bias are at the other.

Self-evaluation. Scriven (1994) also believes that teachers should self-evaluate in the name of accountability. "Accountability obliges you to be able to demonstrate that success to third parties . . . and hence that you are in fact successful" (p. 159). Evaluation is done to serve the public interest where students, parents and taxpayers are the clients, stakeholders and consumers of evaluation (Alkin & Christie, 2004).

Self-evaluation in teacher evaluation is the process to judge one's worth, usually by rating elements of teaching on the district's instrument. For example, Marzano et al. (2020) recommend that teachers rate themselves at least once a year on tendencies of current teaching practices. And while self-evaluation requires some amount of reflection, they differ in purpose, process, and audience. Self-evaluation is justification for the purpose of accountability for a public audience, while reflection is inquiry for the purpose of learning. Reflection is a way of learning from what we do, experience, and understand about any knowledge or teaching method we are using. It is a way of rigorously examining our actions and decisions and improving the overall quality of our work (Arredondo Rucinski, 2005, p. 79). Therefore, in self-evaluation teachers demonstrate that they are successful by assembling evidence in a portfolio and rating themselves to be accountable to their many publics.

Goal-free, but needs-based. The evaluator must collect evidence to assess a lesson's outcomes, any unintended consequences, and whether the lesson addresses the needs of students (Stufflebeam, 2013). Thus, the evaluator enters the evaluation with limited information about the lesson's purpose and student abilities. The evaluator can hypothesize the purpose of the lesson, collect related evidence, and then discuss this evidence in the post-conference to determine whether the teacher accomplished the lesson purpose. So, without pre-knowledge of the lesson, the evaluator is in the best position to determine its outcomes and any unintended consequences.

Generic and particularized. Scholars (and entrepreneurs) of teacher evaluation, influenced by the process-product research, have promoted the generic teacher in instruments and workshops but ignored the particular. Generic criteria have prevailed, so that principals, lacking content expertise, have the legitimacy needed to evaluate teachers (Hazi, 2019a). Thinking about the generic teacher has persisted, despite the emerging research (content pedagogy) that content and context do matter (Lochmiller, 2019). Indeed, Scriven believes there must be *both* generic and particularized criteria for evaluating teachers (Stufflebeam, 2013) because some duties are common to all teachers, while particular duties are teacher-specific to subject, grade level, lesson, and context (Hazi 2019a). For example, classroom management and classroom climate are considered generic, while asking questions and facilitating discussions are considered subject-specific (Hill & Grossman, 2013).

Multiple methods and sources of evidence. Principal observation was the primary method to evaluate until Gates' Measures of Effective Teaching Project reminded educators that multiple methods are best (Hazi, 2019a). More data and more rigorous data from multiple sources are assumed important to the annual evaluation of veteran teachers that may only happen once a year. In addition to principal observation, multiple measures of student growth, student surveys, and student learning objectives were re-discovered (Hazi, 2019a). Evidence includes a teacher's portfolio, subject-matter competence, student ratings of instruction, lesson plans, worksheets, and a sample of student work, along with tests and grades (Scriven, 1994). These examples tend to be used informally by teachers in their improvement of practice.

Utility. Since the 1960s and 1970s, leader workshops have focused on teaching about an instrument and developing accuracy in its use. Accuracy is established by inter-rater reliability. Raters can achieve sufficient levels of inter-rater reliability "after a good deal of training in coding the behaviors" (Berliner, 2018, p. 11–12). However, Scriven believes that utility trumps accuracy. Utility is the "extent to which an evaluation serves the relevant information needs of evaluatees and other users" (Joint Committee on Standards for Educational Evaluation, 2009, p. 197). Unfortunately, most evaluations conducted do little to improve teaching practice. Above all, evaluation must be useful to those evaluated, even above accuracy (Stufflebeam, 2013). Only recently have researchers focused on whether teachers find their evaluations useful (e.g., Donaldson, 2021).

PRINCIPLES FOR GUIDING PRACTICE

As leaders begin to reconsider their practice and management of teacher evaluation, they need to revise policy so that it can address the principles thus far presented. In some cases, they may not be able to do so because they are bound by regulation, statute, or collective bargaining agreement. If this is the case, advocacy through professional organizations can educate and influence boards of education or state legislators. In the meantime, the three principles that follow will ensure that leaders focus evaluation on what teachers need to be participants in, and not objects of, accountability.

A seat at the table. Teachers have been objects of teacher evaluation rather than participants. "Principals deliver feedback to teachers" is an oft-accepted assumption in many teacher evaluation discourses (Hazi, 2019b) as well as in the research on feedback. More is written about how to give feedback than how teachers use feedback to improve (Hazi, 2020; Winstone et al., 2017). However, teachers need to have a seat at the table as districts and states revise teacher evaluation policy. Teacher participation is overlooked not because of malicious intent, but rather due to lack of time, not knowing how, or fear of losing power. Behrstock-Sherratt et al. (2013) claim that authentic teacher participation can create shared ownership, legitimacy, smoother implementation, and help in problem-solving in teacher evaluation.

As the COVID pandemic forced teachers to online instruction, some of the larger school districts in the United States wisely negotiated memoranda of understanding with their teachers. These memoranda were short-term fixes to collective bargaining contracts on issues of most concern to both teachers and leaders, especially a waiver from or an abbreviation of their evaluation (Hemphill & Marianno, 2021). In the 2020–21 school year, some school district memoranda provided for remote observations of teachers and changes in their frequency, timing, and formality (Saenz-Armstrong, 2021). Teachers need to participate in determining all aspects of their evaluation.

Focus on teacher learning. Teacher evaluation has focused on principal learning about an instrument and helping them "deliver feedback." It has been principal-centric (Hazi, 2021). Such a focus has been a traditional and simplistic approach to instructional improvement where the teacher is expected to act on feedback and that a change in teacher behavior is an indicator of improvement. Teacher evaluation needs to focus on teaching and teacher learning and be teacher-centric (Hazi 2020, 2021).

The evaluation instrument is assumed to house most of the information principals need to know about teaching. However, an instrument usually promotes a single model of teaching. In the 1980s it was Madeline Hunter's 7 step model of direct teaching. In the 2000s it was Charlotte Danielson's constructivist model of teaching (Hazi, 2019a). However, these instruments tend to parse teaching into "small bits" that are visible and "generic" behaviors that most teachers engage in regardless of subject, grade level, lesson, or abilities of students (Kennedy, 2016).

Principals are trained to be accurate (reliable). Once trained, they are re-trained and monitored (calibrated) to ensure fidelity to the instrument, so that principals will not "drift" away from the fixed meaning of behaviors (Youngs & Grissom, 2016). Principals are also trained to use "soft language" in conferences so that teachers can buy-in to the process (Hazi, 2019b). "The evaluator's feedback, based on this instrument, is presumed to be correct and what the teacher needs" (Hazi, 2019b, p. 161). Because behaviors are taken out of contexts, teachers may not find the feedback as useful (Hazi, 2020) and may require situated knowledge (Sykes, 1999), especially with the growing findings of pedagogical content knowledge (e.g., McConachie & Petrosky, 2010).

If professional development focused on teaching, more time would focus on understanding a variety of effective teaching situations, rather than a single model of teaching. If teacher evaluation focused on teacher learning, more time would focus on helping teachers to study their teaching to determine how students are mastering the content and what techniques seem to work. Teachers and principals should attend professional development together.

Focus on judgment. Principal workshops focus on an instrument and on how to fit the teacher to it—not on how to see in classrooms, collect evidence, and judge teaching. Looking in classrooms is complex; yet an instrument's rubric may overly simplify this task. A rubric appears to be comprehensive, clear, precise, objective, easy to use, and trustworthy (Hazi 2019a). Many teachers and principals evaluate a rubric positively; but are unable to show improvements to instruction (Donaldson, 2021). This disconnect suggests that rubrics may clarify expectations on how to get a higher observation score, but may have little relationship to improving instruction in classrooms. Training helps principals learn to "match the performance to the description rather than judge it" (Brookhart, 2013, p. 4; Hazi, 2019a, 2019b).

Judgment "is a peculiar talent which can be practiced only and cannot be taught" (Kant's 1781 *Critique of Pure Reason* as cited in Procee, 2006). Cogan (1973, p. 39), influenced by positivism and the sciences, believed that individuals needed to know and control their biases "to make professionally defensible decisions." The individual must be open, flexible, and examine one's judgments so that the observer not be "judgmental," nor "judge rigidly or too rapidly" (p. 41). At the time, judgment was believed to be strongly influenced and limited by perception and frame of mind. The remedy then was to train observers to control their biases and to see and to videotape so that the teacher could participate in the process. Judgment requires evidence that includes "stable data" such as videos, and avoiding premature judgment (Cogan, 1973; Garman, 1986).

Teachers and leaders must find ways to think about core practices of teaching within different subjects and their apparent purposes (Kennedy, 2016), rather than parsing practice into small bits of discrete behaviors that are generic and less useful to teachers. Principals should have opportunities to observe then discuss the purpose of the lesson, whether the lesson accomplished its purpose, and what evidence supports that judgment in a "think aloud" setting. Here principals can learn from others that there are different approaches to judging (Hazi & Arredondo Rucinski, 2016), multiple interpretations of seeing what occurs in classrooms, and many ways that teachers can help students learn.

CONCLUSION

Teacher evaluation in the United States has been buffeted by many forces in hopes of "getting teacher evaluation right" (Darling-Hammond, 2013). Getting it "right" is more aspirational than achievable. Rather than stay locked into practices that result in little progress, we should reconsider these principles of evaluation that are foundations for practice: the formative and summative; distancing; self-evaluation; goal-free, but needs-based; generic and particularized; multiple methods and sources of evidence; and utility. In any changes to evaluation, we should make sure teachers have a seat at the table, that their learning is our goal, and that professional development includes the study of teaching and judgment. These are imperatives for managing the learning process for teachers in the 21st century. We should focus less on teacher control and disempowerment and more on teacher learning. If our goal is teacher quality, teachers should be full participants in evaluation that is teacher-centric.

CASE STUDY QUESTIONS

These questions may require further investigation starting with references cited in the chapter.

1. Your district decides to develop a new rubric to evaluate teachers in this hybrid learning environment, especially as some hope to continue some version of this in the post-pandemic future. As a principal, what is your position about this, and what do you advise your superintendent about its development process and product?
2. You've been asked to participate in a team to negotiate teacher evaluation. Knowing your challenges and inherent problems, what aspects do you want to bring to the table? What aspects are non-negotiable, and where are you willing to compromise?
3. Evaluate your district's teacher evaluation and identify the evaluation principles and practices that are reflected in your policy and instrument. What would you have to do to integrate the remaining principles? What process would have to exist to go about this?
4. Your school system has been introduced to Improvement Science. Two of your teachers, excited in doing a lesson study in mathematics, come to ask your advice about how they could get started and use their work in their evaluation. Having read about this evolving movement in your doctoral program, you begin to see that teacher discussions could occur in the

same grade level, across schools, or in the same subject across districts, in many imaginable combinations. These networks could constitute "safe space" where teachers disclose information that will help them set goals for improvement. Should you encourage a process that is separate from or connected to their evaluation, especially when you see the rich evidence that comes from those networks and housed in teacher portfolios? How do you make this decision?

NOTES

1. An earlier version of this chapter was a paper presented at the annual meeting of the Council of Professors of Instructional Supervision.

2. I differentiate evaluation from supervision which are similar, yet not identical. Supervision is a practice to help teachers to inquire into and to make progress in their teaching. They are similar because both require evidence from the classroom and involve judgment. They differ in their practice and dilemmas, yet they are forever entangled as fraternal twins in the minds and practice of educators (Hazi, 1994, 2012).

REFERENCES

Alkin, M., & Christie, C. (2004). An evaluation theory tree. In M. Alkin (Ed.), *Evaluation roots: Tracing theorists' views and influences* (pp. 12–65). Sage.

Arredondo Rucinski, D. (2005). Standards for reflective practice. In S. Gordon (Ed.), *Standards for instructional supervision: Enhancing teaching and learning* (pp. 77–90). Eye on Education.

Behrstock-Sherratt, E., Rizzolo, A., Laine, S., & Friedman, W. (2013). *Everyone at the table: Engaging teachers in evaluation reform*. Jossey-Bass.

Berliner, D. (2018). Between Scylla and Charybdis: Reflections on and problems associated with the evaluation of teachers in an era of metrification. *Education Policy Analysis Archives, 26*(54), 1–24. https://epaa.asu.edu/ojs/article/view/3820.

Brookhart, S. (2013). *How to create and use rubrics for formative assessment and grading*. Association for Supervision and Curriculum Development.

Bryk, A. S. (2015). 2014 AERA Distinguished lecture: Accelerating how we learn to improve. *Education Researcher, 44*(9), 467–477. https://doi.org/10.3102/0013189X15621543.

Cogan, M. (1973). *Clinical supervision*. Houghton Mifflin.

Darling-Hammond, L. (2013). *Getting teacher evaluation right: What really matters for effectiveness and improvement*. Teachers College Press.

Donaldson, M. (2021). *Multidisciplinary perspectives on teacher evaluation: Understanding the research and theory*. Routledge.

Every Student Succeeds Act, 20 U.S.C. § 6301 (2015). https://www.congress.gov/bill/114th-congress/senate-bill/1177.

Garman, N.B. (1986). Clinical supervision: Quackery or remedy for professional practice. *Journal of Curriculum and Supervision, 1*(2), 148–157.

Hazi, H. M. (1994). The teacher evaluation-supervision dilemma: A case of entanglements and irreconcilable differences. *Journal of Curriculum and Supervision, 9*(2), 195–216. http://www.ascd.org/publications/jcs/winter1994/The_Teacher_Evaluation-Supervision_Dilemma@_A_Case_of_Entanglements_and_Irreconcilable_Differences.aspx.

Hazi, H. M. (2012). *Expert judgment: A concept for teacher evaluation in a post-modern world.* A paper presented at the annual meeting of the American Educational Research Association, Vancouver, British Columbia.

Hazi, H. M. (2014). The marketing of teacher evaluation: The seductive claims of instruments. *The WERA Educational Journal 6*(1), 2–9.

Hazi, H. M. (2019a). Coming to understand the wicked problem of teacher evaluation. In S. J. Zepeda & J. Ponticell (Eds.), *Handbook of educational supervision* (pp. 183–207). Wiley-Blackwell.

Hazi, H. M. (2019b). The language of instructional improvement in the U.S. In M. L. Derrington & J. Brandon (Eds.), *Differentiated teacher evaluation and professional learning: Policies and practices for promoting career growth* (pp. 149–171). Palgrave Macmillan.

Hazi, H. M. (2020). On instructional improvement: A modest essay. *Journal of Educational Supervision, 3*(3), 90–103. https://digitalcommons.library.umaine.edu/jes/vol3/iss3/7/.

Hazi, H. M. (2021). A swerve in times of crises: Rethinking teacher evaluation anew. In J. Glanz (Ed.), *Crisis and pandemic leadership: Implications for meeting the needs of students, teachers, and parents* (pp. 47–58). Rowman & Littlefield.

Hazi, H. M., & Arredondo Rucinski, D. (2016). Teacher evaluation and professional development: How legal mandates encroach on core principles of supervision. In J. Glanz and S. J. Zepeda (Eds.), *Supervision: New perspectives for theory and practice* (pp. 187–200). Rowman & Littlefield.

Hemphill, A., & Marianno, B. (2021). Teachers unions, collective bargaining, and the response to COVID-19. *Education Finance and Policy, 16*(1), 170–182. https://doi.org/10.1162/edfp_a_00326.

Hiebert, J., & Stigler, J. W. (2017). Teaching versus teachers as a lever for change: Comparing a Japanese and a U.S. perspective on improving instruction. *Educational Researcher, 46*(4), 169–176. https://doi.org/10.3102/0013189X17711899.

Hill, H., & Grossman, P. (2013). Learning from teacher observations: Challenges and opportunities posed by new teacher evaluation system. *Harvard Educational Review, 83*(2), 371–384. https://doi.org/10.17763/haer.83.2.d11511403715u376.

Hunter, M. (1988). Effecting a reconciliation between supervision and evaluation—A reply to Popham. *Journal of Personnel Evaluation in Education, 1*(3), 275–279. https://doi: 10.1007/BF00123823.

Joint Committee on Standards for Educational Evaluation, The. (2009). *The personnel evaluation standards: How to assess systems for evaluating educators.* Corwin

Kennedy, M. (2016). Parsing the practice of teaching. *Journal of Teacher education, 67*(1), 6–17. https://doi 10.1177/0022487115614617.

Kraft, M., Blazar, D., & Hogan, D. (2018). The effect of teacher coaching on instruction and achievement: A meta-analysis of the causal evidence. *Review of Educational Research, 88*(4), 547–588. http://doi10.3102/0034654318759268.

Lasch, C. (1978). *The culture of narcissism: American life in an age of diminishing expectations.* W.W. Norton.

LeMahieu, P., Grunow, A., Baker L., Nordstrum, L., & Gomez, L. (2017). Networked improvement communities: The discipline of improvement science meets the power of networks. *Quality Assurance in Education, 25*(1), 5–25. www.emeraldinsight.com/0968-4883.htm.

Leahy, C. (2012). *Teacher evaluation training: Ensuring quality classroom observers.* Education Commission of the States. http://www.ecs.org/clearinghouse/01/01/14/10114.pdf.

Lochmiller, C. R. (2019). Credibility in instructional supervision: Catalyst for differentiation. In M. L. Derrington & J. Brandon (Eds.), *Differentiated teacher evaluation and professional learning: Policies and practices for promoting career growth* (pp. 83–105). Palgrave Macmillan.

McConachie, S., & Petrosky, A. (2010). *Content matters: A disciplinary literacy approach to improving student learning.* Jossey-Bass.

Marzano, R. (2012). The two purposes of teacher evaluation. *Educational Leadership, 70*(3), 14–19. http://www.ascd.org/publications/educational-leadership/nov12/vol70/num03/The-Two-Purposes-of-Teacher-Evaluation.aspx.

Marzano, R., Rains, C., & Warrick, P. (2020). *Improving teacher development and evaluation.* Marzano Resources.

Pajak, E. (2011). Cultural narcissism and education reform. *Teachers College Record, 113*(9), 2018–2046. https://www.tcrecord.org/content.asp?contentid=16181.

Popham, W. J. (1988). The dysfunctional marriage of formative and summative teacher evaluation. *Journal of Personnel Evaluation in Education, 1*(3), 269–273. https://doi:10.1007/BF00123822.

Popham, W. J. (2013). On serving two masters: formative and summative teacher evaluation. *Principal Leadership, 13*(7), 18–22. http://www.nassp.org/Content/158/PLmar13_popham.pdf.

Procee, H. (2006). Reflection in education: A Kantian epistemology. Educational Theory, 56(3), 237–253. http://10.1111/j.1741-5446.2006.00225.x.

Reinhorn, S., Moore Johnson, S., & Simon, N. (2017). Investing in development: Six high-performing, high-poverty schools implement the Massachusetts teacher evaluation policy. *Educational Evaluation and Policy Analysis, 39*(3), 383–406. https://doi.org/10.3102/0162373717690605.

Saenz-Armstrong, P. (2021, January 14). Tracking district teacher policies in the COVID-19 environment. National Council on Teacher Quality. https://www.nctq.org/blog/Tracking-district-teacher-policies-in-the-COVID—19 environment.?utm_source=NCTQ+Newsletters+and+Announcements&utm_campaign=093aab7752-Trendline+1.14.21&utm_medium=email&utm_term=0_06ef29c06d-093aab7752-409204306.

Schaffhauser, D. (2020, August 31). Rubric helps districts identify areas of improvement for fall return. *The Journal.* https://thejournal.com/articles/2020/08/31/rubric-helps-districts-identify-areas-of-improvement-for-fall-return.aspx.

Scriven, M. (1967). The methodology of evaluation. In R.W. Tyler, R. W. Gagne, & M. Scriven (Eds.), *American Educational Research Association monograph series on curriculum evaluation: Vol. 1. Perspectives of curriculum evaluation*. Rand McNally.

Scriven, M. (1994). Duties of a teacher. *Journal of Personnel Evaluation in Education, 8*(2), 151–184. https://doi.org/10.1007/BF00972261.

Scriven, M. (1996). Truth and objectivity in evaluation. *Evaluation for the 21st century: A handbook* (pp. 477–500). Sage.

Stufflebeam, D. (2013). My tribute to a trail blazer: Evaluation iconoclast—Professor Michael Scriven. *The future of evaluation in society: A tribute to Michael Scriven* (pp. 73–91). Information Age.

Sykes, G. (1999). Teacher and student learning: Strengthening their connection. In L. Darling-Hammond & G. Sykes (Eds.), *Teaching as the learning profession: Handbook of policy and practice* (pp. 151–179). John Wiley & Sons.

Williams. T. (2020, August 5). How to evaluate teachers during remote learning, and other advice for principals. *Education Week*. https://www.edweek.org/ew/articles/2020/08/06/how-to-evaluate-teachers-during-remote-learning.html?cmp=eml-enl-eu-news2&M=59640332&U=&UUID=5db99379423bd8f2b72457b68b37431b.

Winstone, N.E., Nash, R.A., Parker, M., & Rowntree, J. (2017). Supporting learners' agentic engagement with feedback: A systematic review and a taxonomy of recipience processes. *Educational Psychologist, 52*(1), 17–37. https://doi10.1080/00461520.2016.1207538.

Youngs, P. & Grissom, J. A. (2016). Multiple measures in teacher evaluation; Lessons learned and guidelines for practice (pp. 169–183). In. J. A. Grissom & P. Youngs (Eds.), *Improving teacher evaluation systems: Making the most of multiple measures*. Teachers College Press.

Chapter Five

Managing School Safety

Boundary Management within a Bourdieu Framework

Pascale Benoliel

INTRODUCTION

School managers in the 21st century are often faced with seemingly intractable problems. Schools have experienced global and technological challenges that generations heretofore never had to encounter. Given unprecedented internal and external pressures, leaders, especially in their management capacities, must be creative and entrepreneurial. They must be able to manage internal and external settings simultaneously with efficiently (Adams & Muthiah, 2020). This chapter will explore the complex personal and contextual challenges experienced by school stakeholders from a unique theoretical lens (Bourdieu, 1986). Managing school safety will be the primary, not only, issue the chapter will address.

A fundamental concern for schools worldwide is how to best develop students' sense of safety to support both their academic performance and their mental health. Therefore, schools and their leaders have a special responsibility to meaningfully and routinely support their students' feeling of safety in the school (Theron, 2016). Despite interventions and procedures intended to ensure school safety, events involving verbal and physical acts of violence persist and even appear to be on the rise (Povedano et al., 2015; Yablon, 2019).

Research has shown that students' behavioral issues are the result of the interaction between individuals and their families and schools (Kangas-Dick & O'Shaughnessy, 2020). Studies have highlighted the importance of social bonding as an important way to decrease student disruptive behaviors, while also supporting student academic achievement (Cristall et al., 2020). For instance, caring and supportive teachers and principals who function as mentors and role models or builders of positive relationships are essential for improving school safety (Liebenberg et al., 2016). Therefore, a successful approach to school safety would seem to require a perspective that identifies every facet of the school body. Such a systemic perspective to school safety should consider the characteristics of the school's internal and external environments, which would include essential school stakeholders and faculty. A systemic approach can not only address disruptive behavior by students generally but can also consider the basic structures of the school environment that may facilitate or constrain the application of procedures aimed at reducing such behavior.

Empirical research has shown that successful principals create conditions that promote a safe school environment, along with effective teaching and learning (Hallinger, 2018; Sun & Leithwood, 2017). However, most studies have emphasized the conditions that promote or hinder the success of programs aimed at preventing school violence, exclusively focusing on the individual students (Fletcher et al., 2015; Yablon & Addington, 2018). This chapter focuses on principals as important agents for enlarging the school's social capital (i.e., its actual and potential resources within a given social context) and the role of the principal's boundary activities (i.e., building and maintaining of social relationships within and beyond the school) in promoting school safety.

Accordingly, this chapter seeks to acknowledge the challenge for principals associated with managing the school boundary and maintaining a good balance between the school's internal processes and the school's external environment requirements. Too much of the educational leadership literature continues to focus on either the individual or individuals. In contrast, this chapter is premised on the idea put forth by Bourdieu that human actions occur within fields of interaction (Bourdieu, 1977, 1990; Bourdieu & Wacquant, 1992). Therefore, the proposed boundary-spanning approach to school leadership focuses on the role of situation in leadership practice.

The school context encompasses the networks for students, teachers, principals, and external stakeholders (Benoliel, 2020; Leithwood, Harris & Hopkins, 2020). The possibility of resource transfers in the form of social capital is contingent upon the design, quantity, and value of social relationships in the professional network (Coleman, 1988). School social capital may be demonstrated by effective boundary management on the part of the principals, which in turn contributes to improving the school safety climate. In other words, knowledge sharing and social relationships in a social and professional network can be improved by principals, who are well-positioned to function as agents for positive change through their boundary activities. Again, while the concept of social capital focuses on the potential of social relationships for acquiring resources, boundary management involves the building and maintaining of social relationships within and across the boundary.

PROMOTING SCHOOL SAFETY THROUGH BOURDIEU'S FRAMEWORK

As a result of continuous reforms and increased community involvement in the school decision-making process, principals are increasingly responsible for shaping and improving the conditions for a safe school learning environment (Benoliel, 2020; Hallinger, 2018). Maintaining and promoting school safety is important for several reasons. First, school safety is correlated to student learning and academic achievement. Research points to positive correlations between a safe school climate and improved school achievement (Cohen et al., 2019; Shapira-Lishchinsky, 2018). Second, research suggests that safety, both inside and outside the school context, is an important indicator of student well-being (Yablon & Addington, 2018). Third, low school safety can be costly to school systems, and can negatively influence teacher well-being and morale (Burton & Leoschut, 2013; Skaalvik & Skaalvik, 2017; Varela et al., 2018). Finally, low levels of school safety may produce instability, with implications for the level of learning and instruction (Valois et al., 2012).

Several barriers can restrict the development of a holistic perspective toward school safety. First, the school structure and schoolwork arrangement are still described as a loosely coupled structure with weak relationships among teachers, who stay relatively independent within their classrooms (Weick, 2009). Thus, teachers primarily learn from personal experiences (Senge, 2012). Second, since schools belong to the broader environments within which they operate, the culture of schools relative to school safety is subject to the environmental definition of school safety standards by the school's external stakeholders (parents, community, district, government) (Giles & Hargreaves, 2006; Fischman et al., 2019). The growth of school size and an increasingly test-based accountability environment have turned schools into open systems in transactional relationships with their resource-providing environments (Addi-Raccah, 2019). Since school boundaries are permeable, principals are exposed to and pressured to conform to the external influences of their environments.

Bourdieu's (1986) approach is useful to more fully understand the interaction between the boundary-spanning practices of a principal with a particular *"habitus"* working across several fields with different power structures, hierarchies, and logics of practice (e.g., financial and political measures of success) because it provides insight regarding the different establishments and individuals situated within a system of relationships with an encompassing logic of action. It is concerning particular fields of practice that the habitus develops and a person's habitus can be more or less appropriate to the demands of a specific field.

Bourdieu's notions of *"habitus"* and *"field,"* when used in the framework of leadership research, enable us to highlight the recurrent association between agency (individual leader habitus) and structure (field) in the larger social environment. *"Habitus"* enables us to perceive the leader above his or her effect, concentrating on the relation to particular social structures and personal predispositions. *"Field"* enables us to focus on the leadership context, that is, the school, considered as 'structured social space' with its own characteristics and power relationships, interconnecting with several fields (e.g., financial, political). Similar to other fields, the educational field encompasses its chain of command and logics of practice and is interrelated to other fields as well (e.g., political, technological, economic), with their own impact on the educational field.

THE FRAMEWORK

We have used Bourdieu's work to study the interplay between the practices of principals with a unique habitus, operating across several fields characterized by various logics of practice, power structures, and chain of command. Bourdieu (1986, 1990) suggests that the interactions across fields are hierarchical and indicated that the economic and political fields affect, in some measure, other less autonomous fields, such as the educational field. For instance, the educational field is relatively weak and its boundaries are increasingly porous (Blackmore, 2010; Bourdieu, 1996) due to the rising pressure of global, political, and economic fields.

Habitus

Bourdieu (in Wacquant, 1989) explains the association between habitus and field as follows: either as conditioning, where the field constructs the habitus, or as a cognitive construction in which the habitus also participates in structuring the field. Consequently, habitus offers a means to understand how the social world is personified, influencing how individuals perceive, think, and behave. Habitus provides a language to explain the tension between the way the system influences individual actions and perceptions, and the possibility for exerting agency. Bourdieu presents the habitus as both a "structured-structure" (produced by the environment and the principal) and a "structuring-structure" (influencing the principal's understanding and behavior). Habitus is useful, then, to illustrate the development of principals concerning the school context, circumstances, and social procedures in their environment. The habitus, which is defined by the environment in which the principal works, restricts the principal's action and autonomy, and requires a variety of attitudes that result from the embodiment of the social context in which they arise.

Field

According to Bourdieu, the social world consists of some diverse social "fields" in which conflicts take place over particular interests. Fields have distinct logics, structures, and regulations that manage them. Fields also consist of social positions and the interactions among the different positions. Depending upon the level of interest, positions within the field may be filled by individual social agents (e.g., principals, teachers) or the organization (e.g., schools). Power dynamics in fields of practice derive from the relative status of various agents (Bourdieu & Wacquant, 1992). Research endorses the suggestion that "cross-field effects" may result from the interactions between the practices (Rawolle, 2010). Consequently, students, principals, and schools are situated in a "structured social space" characterized by other forms of power, correlating with economic, political, and other factors (Spillane et al., 2001).

Field effects may also correlate to the forms of autonomy available within a field, and how status and power are recognized within a field (Rawolle & Lingard, 2013). Thus, the magnitude of a field's autonomy is displayed by the strength of its ability to divert inference from other fields, specifically the political and economic fields. In the context of this chapter, "field" refers to the education system, and more specifically the environment that restrains individual schools' and their leaders' ways of "playing the game." The field thus produces the boundaries within which students, teachers, leaders, and schools behave daily.

Social Capital

Bourdieu's view of social capital highlights conflicts and the power of the role/function of an agent, that is, social relationships can improve the capacity of an agent to promote his/her interests. According to the Bourdieu point of view, social capital becomes a resource in the social efforts engaged within the various fields of practice. Putnam (2001, p. 19) concentrates on the reciprocally advantageous characteristics of the relationship defining social capital as "connections among individuals—social networks and the norms of reciprocity and trustworthiness that arise from them." From these perspectives, the notion of member interaction that enables the establishment and maintenance of rooted "social" resources is emphasized. The essential and stable definition of social capital centers on resources embedded in social relationships and social networks (Lin & Erickson, 2008).

Thomson (2001) points out that principals, positioned as they are at the intersection between several fields, must navigate several logics of practice. This tends to diminish their ability to determine their standards for safety and school effectiveness, affecting their *habitus*. For instance, the instructional and pedagogical culture of schools is largely subject to the external requirements for success embodied by standardized tests as well as policy requirements imposed by external stakeholders (school districts, government) that tend to define school effectiveness according to student achievements (Kruse, 2018; Leithwood et al., 2017). Thus, organizational structures, policies, and procedures can discourage principals from implementing school-specific procedures for school safety. In addition, the educational field is sculpted by socio-historical disparities that compel schools and their leaders to "play the game" the way other schools do, yet sometimes with fewer resources. Bourdieu explains "games" as follows: there are "stakes" (*enjeux*) that are mostly a result of the competition among various actors.

Principals are vulnerable to external factors that can threaten the school and harm the principal's professional standing (Addi-Raccah et al., 2018; Johnson & Fauske, 2000). Principals have to market the school to obtain legitimacy for their actions and guarantee the flow of resources to the school. Gewirtz and her colleagues (1995) refer to the "glossification" of schools; despite whatever obstacles exist, the best possible image for the school must be displayed to the outside world. The principal is also positioned at the boundary between the school and the local community, with its own logic of practices and expectations (Valli et al., 2018). For example, parental involvement in students' learning and school-home relationships based on respect and cooperation are related to positive school learning outcomes and student well-being (Epstein et al., 2018; Povey et al., 2016).

In another study, Dawson-McClure et al. (2017) indicated that parental intervention as a part of the school program was essential for reaching families and dealing with student academic and behavioral issues. Repeated exchanges of social and cultural capital (Bourdieu, 1986) with several communities can promote partnership growth through various learning experiences. However, in the school context, there is also another logic of practice associated with the establishment of instructional practices and assessments and the establishment of school values, policies, and structures related to these (Lingard et al., 2003).

While principals have some level of autonomy within their schools, they are subject to pressures exerted by the school environment and thus become the players who develop tactics to "play the game" according to their habitus and their understanding of the dominant narratives. Thus principals, through their positions and their experience at "playing the game," tend to behave according to the rules of the game and their habitus. For example, principals who are predisposed to emphasize school achievement in terms of effectiveness and safety play the game to maintain their professional position and perhaps to enlarge their capital.

Tactically, this kind of "playing the game" can involve both external and internal boundary activities. Therefore, the principal's boundary management activities may reflect a logical field practice, performed to guarantee that school "players" (teachers and students) also adapt to the logic of the field. Concurrently, they act to maintain and promote the school's position and their own position within the field. The principal's boundary-spanning role is therefore situated in a structured social space in which the role itself is subject to potentially contradictory basic assumptions. On one hand, there is an internal perspective, the *habitus*, focused on educational practices. On the other hand, there is the external perspective focused on economic, political, and global measures of success.

PRINCIPAL BOUNDARY MANAGEMENT ACROSS SEVERAL FIELDS OF PRACTICE INCLUDING SCHOOL SAFETY

Successful principals must be skilled at balancing competing demands arising from new political and economic pressures (e.g., standardized testing requirements and distribution of monies from a district office). At the same time, they must be able to act according to the codified rules of audit, management, and markets which individualize, the performance of each teacher, each principal, and each school (Thomson, 2010). Since school subsystems are structured to interact and influence the whole system, continuous efficient interaction of the different school components is essential, requiring flexibility and rapid adaptation to new situations and contexts (Bridwell-Mitchell, 2018).

Research confirms that schools are sometimes less aware of the knowledge, skills, and culture rooted in their surrounding communities (Wrigley, 2003), potentially producing a misfit regarding appropriate norms and expectations. Principals need to understand the forces influencing the behavior of students and faculty, seeing the whole picture to reach within by connecting to the expectations and visions of the school body (Shaked, 2018; Shaked & Benoliel, 2020).

Individuals engaging in boundary activities (i.e., negotiating potentially competing internal and external demands) have been referred to by Cohen and Levinthal (1990) as "gatekeepers," or "boundary spanners." These individuals (in our context principals) transform the resources acquired from external partnerships into assets for organizational improvement. An important task for principals is to not only meet local, social, political, and global demands but also to preserve the acquired resources to meet the needs of school faculty and thus students by enabling the school's ongoing educational activities (Lingard & Lewis, 2016; Thomson, 2010). Principals thus span the school boundary, building and maintaining positive partnerships with external stakeholders to obtain legitimacy for their instructional and managerial activities and also to acquire the numerous resources needed for their survival (Valli et al., 2018; Wang, 2018).

Recent research has shown that in their role as boundary managers, today's principals devote much attention to boundary management, engaging in internal and external boundary activities aimed at guaranteeing that the school boundary is neither too tightly delineated nor too permeable (Benoliel, 2017; Shaked & Benoliel, 2020). On the one hand, through internal boundary activities, principals can tighten the boundary around the school, building trust, and promoting a sense of belonging to and identification with the school's instructional goals as well as protecting school faculty from external pressures (Benoliel, 2017). On the other hand, by loosening the boundary around the school through external boundary activities, principals can scout for new resources, mobilize support and legitimacy, and monitor changes in the school environment that could potentially impact the school's educational processes (Addi-Raccah, 2015).

Following the Druskat and Wheeler (2003) typology, adapted for schools by Benoliel (2017, 2020), principal boundary activities involve the internal and external activities, referred to above. *Internal boundary activities* are those activities that involve internal school matters occurring within the school boundary and include: (a) *Relating*—building trust among faculty staff and showing care for school faculty. Trust encourages the school's administration and staff to share more precise information about issues, to give essential feedback, and to engage in challenging conversations (Tschannen-Moran, 2014; Edmondson, 2012). (b) *Scouting*—meeting faculty needs and assisting them to solve their pedagogical issues. (c) *Persuading*—persuading faculty to set priorities that are in line with the school's goals and to create a common vision. (d) *Empowering*—delegating authority and mobilizing leadership capacity at all school levels to improve the learning climate. For example, research (Goddard et al., 2015; Gregory et al., 2012) has shown that schools characterized by high levels of collaboration experience less school violence than bureaucratically structured schools.

External boundary activities are activities aimed at representing the school to external constituents, gaining access to resources and external support, and scanning the environment for information and knowledge necessary for meeting school goals (Benoliel, 2020). External activities include: (a) *Relating*—building and maintaining positive relationships between the school and external stakeholders. (b) *Scouting*—searching for knowledge and resources from external sources. (c) *Persuading*—obtaining external support for the schools' mission and goals. For example, research has shown that school leaders work to cultivate parental support by involving family members in developing workshops, providing tutoring, and assisting teachers in classrooms or with after-school activities (Dipaola & Tschannen-Moran, 2005). Therefore, schools absorb elements from the environment to reduce threats by exchanging some degree of control, including control of information, in return for the commitment of continued support from the community.

CONCLUSION

Principals' performance of their role is rooted in their habitus (Bourdieu, 1990) that provides the "logic of practice" for their day-to-day work. The habitus is subject to negotiation and change, rooted in the power relationships that function in the field of practice. Schools can be seen as structured social spaces with their own "logics" of practice. There is a multitude of fields and social relations. As the pressures and requirements on school leadership become most intense, balancing the opinions of many and achieving a satisfying outcome can be a challenging task. This can be intensified within the context of conflicting requirements from the various stakeholders, particularly in the case of very disadvantaged communities, where many of the school conditions (i.e., capital and related dispositions) are sub-standard.

However, habitus, field of practices, and social capital are intimately connected in determining courses of action and best practices. In schools, such practices develop in the dynamics that emerge between the field players: principals, teachers, students, and their parents, and the school community. These dynamics are in turn dominated by the players' (agent) abilities to organize various kinds of capital, providing the acceptance to respect, privilege, and esteem. Principals are conscious of their position as well as of others.

Principals are responsible for negotiating between competing logics of practice. Thus, the principal's boundary activities take place in fields of practice. Through these boundary activities, principals are continuously involved in influencing these fields of practice as well as the boundaries that separate these fields.

This chapter emphasized the tensions that exist as the principal navigates between transformation and preservation of the "field." These originate from community dynamics, both inside and outside the school, as well as national-level policies. These tensions are rooted in structural-level dynamics in the field of action as well as principal' habitus and practices. They manage the school boundary by building relationships with external stakeholders characterized by their hierarchies and logics of practice.

By engaging in internal and external boundary activities, principals can accommodate and adapt to outside requirements while maintaining the school field by promoting a vision and identity for the school from the inside. Accordingly, a principal can operate as a liaison between the school and school staff on the one hand, and the school's external environment on the other. Through boundary management, principals can balance conflicting and sometimes incompatible demands resulting from new policies or global pressures, while at the same time ensuring that teaching aligns with their vision for the school (Shaked & Benoliel, 2020). The principal's challenge is to build and maintain positive connections across various fields to build up the school's social capital and promote a safe school environment.

CASE STUDY

Dr. Mario Rodriguez is the new principal of an inner-city elementary school. The school has been beset by numerous school safety problems including school violence in the upper grades and a rash of car thefts in the neighborhood in which several teachers' cars were vandalized and/or stolen. Other internal and external safety issues were common. Dr. Rodriguez, an experienced principal with 15 years prior experience, has been charged to handle the internal and external challenges and bring stability to a previously chaotic school environment.

Early on in his new position, Dr. Rodriguez was pressured by teachers to resolve the behavioral issues in the upper grades. Daily physical fights between students and even gang-related acts of violence continued to dominate the educational environment. Violence against teachers, too, was not uncommon. Teachers also complained that they feared for their safety within and outside the school grounds. Parents as well demanded a change. At the district level, the superintendent, although supportive of the new principal, expected results in short order.

What is Dr. Rodriguez to do? This chapter outlined a theoretical framework of boundary management that is important to consider when confronting internal and external challenges. Based on the Bourdieu framework, how would you advise the new principal to navigate between and among the various stakeholders? In what ways would Dr. Rodriguez have to be mindful of "playing the game?" Drawing on the internal and external boundary activities explained in the chapter, what practical strategies would you take to improve school safety in this school and the surrounding community?

REFERENCES

Adams, D., & Muthiah, V. (2020). School principals and 21st century leadership challenges: A systematic review. *Journal of Nusantara Studies, 5*(1), 189–210. https://doi.org/10.24200/jonus.vol5iss1pp189-210.

Addi-Raccah, A. (2015). School principals' role in the interplay between the superintendents and local education authorities: The case of Israel. *Journal of Educational Administration, 53*(2), 287–306. https://doi.org/10.1108/JEA-10-2012-0107.

Addi-Raccah, A. (2019). Private tutoring in a high socio-economic secondary school in Israel and pupils' attitudes towards school learning: A double-edged sword phenomenon. *British Educational Research Journal, 45*(5), 938–960. https://doi.org/10.1002/berj.3545.

Addi-Raccah, A., Amar, J., & Ashwal, Y. (2018). Schools' influence on their environment: The parents' perspective. *Educational Management Administration & Leadership, 46*(5), 782–799. https://doi.org/10.1177%2F1741143217707521.

Benoliel, P. (2017). Managing school management team boundaries and school improvement: An investigation of the school leader role. *International Journal of Leadership in Education, 20*(1), 57–86. https://doi.org/10.1080/13603124.2015.1053536.

Benoliel, P. (2020). Principals' boundary activities and school violence: The mediating role of school management teams. *Educational Management and Administration Leadership, 48*(2), 286–304. https://doi.org/10.1177%2F1741143218802592.

Blackmore, J. (2010). Policy, practice and purpose in the field of education: A critical review. *Critical Studies in Education, 51*(1), 101–111. https://doi.org/10.1080/17508480903450257.

Bourdieu, P. (1977). *Outline of a theory of practice.* Cambridge University Press.

Bourdieu, P. (1986). The forms of capital. In J. Richardson (Ed.), *Handbook of theory and research for the sociology of education* (pp. 241–258). Greenwood.

Bourdieu, P. (1990). *The logic of practice* (R. Nice, trans.). Stanford University Press.

Bourdieu, P. (1996). *The rules of art: Genesis and structure of the literary field*. Stanford University Press.
Bourdieu, P., & Wacquant, L. (1992). *An invitation to reflexive sociology*. Chicago, IL: University of Chicago Press.
Bridwell-Mitchell, E. N. (2018). System self-regulation and static equilibria. In H. Shaked, C. Schechter, & A. Daly (Eds.), *Leading holistically: How schools, districts, and states improve systemically*. Routledge.
Burton, P., & Leoschut, L. (2013). School violence in South Africa. *Results of the 2012 National School Violence Study, Centre for Justice and Crime Prevention, Monograph Series*, No. 12.
Cohen, E., Eshel, Y., Kimhi, S., & Kurman, J. (2019). Individual resilience: a major protective factor in peer bullying and victimization of elementary school children in Israel. *Journal of Interpersonal Violence*, 1–20. https://doi.org/10.1177%2F0886260519863192.
Cohen, W. M., & Levinthal, D. A. (1990). Absorptive capacity: A new perspective on learning and innovation. *Administrative Science Quarterly*, 35(1), 128–152. https://doi.org/10.2307/2393553.
Coleman, J. S. (1988). Social capital in the creation of human capital. *American Journal of Sociology*, 94(1), S95–S120. https://doi.org/10.1086/228943.
Cristall F., Rodger S., Hibbert K. (2020) "Where Love Prevails": Student Resilience and Resistance in Precarious Spaces. In Corbett M., & Gereluk D. (Eds.), *Rural Teacher Education* (155–170). Springer, Singapore. https://doi.org/10.1007/978-981-15-2560-5_7.
Dawson-McClure, S., Calzada, E. J., & Brotman, L. M. (2017). Engaging parents in preventive interventions for young children: Working with cultural diversity within low-income, urban neighborhoods. *Prevention Science*, 18(6), 660–670. https://doi.org/10.1007/s11121-017-0763-7.
DiPaola, M. F., & Tschannen-Moran, M. (2005). Bridging or buffering? The impact of schools' adaptive strategies on student achievement. *Journal of Educational Administration*, 43(1), 60–71. https://doi.org/10.1108/09578230510577290.
Druskat, V. U., & Wheeler, J. V. (2003). Managing from the boundary: The effective leadership of self-managing work teams. *Academy of Management Journal*, 46(4), 435–457. https://doi.org/10.5465/30040637.
Edmondson, A. C. (2012). *Teaming: How organizations learn, innovate, and compete in the knowledge economy*. John Wiley & Sons.
Epstein, J. L., Sanders, M. G., Sheldon, S. B., Simon, B. S., Salinas, K. C., Jansorn, N. R., & Williams, K. J. (2018). *School, family, and community partnerships: Your handbook for action*. Corwin.
Fischman, G. E., Topper, A. M., Silova, I., Goebel, J., & Holloway, J. L. (2019). Examining the influence of international large-scale assessments on national education policies. *Journal of Education Policy*, 34(4), 470–499. https://doi:10.1080/02680939.2018.1460493._
Fletcher, A., Fitzgerald-Yau, N., Wiggins, M., Viner, R. M., & Bonell, C. (2015). Involving young people in changing their school environment to make it safer. *Health Education*, 115(3/4), 322–338. https://doi.org/10.1108/HE-04-2014-0063.

Giles, C., & Hargreaves, A. (2006). The sustainability of innovative schools as learning organizations and professional learning communities during standardized reform. *Educational Administration Quarterly*, *42*(1), 124–156. https://doi.org/10.1177/0013161X05278189.

Gewirtz, S., Ball, S. J., & Bowe, R. (1995). *Markets, choice and equity in education*. Open University Press.

Goddard, R., Goddard, Y., Sook Kim, E., & Miller, R. (2015). A theoretical and empirical analysis of the roles of instructional leadership, teacher collaboration, and collective efficacy beliefs in support of student learning. *American Journal of Education*, *121*(4), 501–530. https://doi.org/10.1086/681925.

Gregory, A., Cornell, D., & Fan, X. (2012). Teacher safety and authoritative school climate in high schools. *American Journal of Education*, *118*(4), 401–425. https://doi.org/10.1086/666362.

Hallinger, P. (2018). Bringing context out of the shadows of leadership. *Educational Management Administration & Leadership*, *46*(1), 5–24. https://doi.org/10.1177%2F1741143216670652.

Johnson Jr., B. L., & Fauske, J. R. (2000). Principals and the political economy of environmental enactment. *Educational Administration Quarterly*, *36*(2), 159–185. https://doi.org/10.1177%2F0013161X00362002.

Kangas-Dick, K., & O'Shaughnessy, E. (2020). Interventions that promote resilience among teachers: A systematic review of the literature. *International Journal of School & Educational Psychology*, *8*(2), 131–146. https://doi.org/10.1080/21683603.2020.1734125.

Kruse, S. (2018). Schools as soft systems: addressing the complexity of ill-defined problems. In H. Shaked, C. Schechter, & A. Daly (Eds). *Leading holistically: How schools, districts, and states improve systemically* (pp. 63–67). Routledge.

Leithwood, K., Harris, A., & Hopkins, D. (2020), "Seven strong claims about successful school leadership revisited," *School Leadership and Management*, *40*(1), pp. 5–22.

Leithwood, K., Sun, J., & Pollock, K. (Eds.). (2017). *How school leaders contribute to student success: The four paths framework* (Vol. 23). Springer. https://doi.org/10.1007/978-3-319-50980-8.

Liebenberg, L., Theron, L., Sanders, J., Munford, R., Van Rensburg, A., Rothmann, S., & Ungar, M. (2016). Bolstering resilience through teacher-student interaction: Lessons for school psychologists. *School Psychology International*, *37*(2), 140–154. https://doi.org/10.1177%2F0143034315614689.

Lin, N., & Erickson, B. H. (2008). Theory, measurement, and the research enterprise on social capital. In Lin, N., & Erickson, B. H. (Eds). *Social capital: An international research program*, (pp. 1–24). Oxford University Press.

Lingard, B., & Lewis, S. (2016). Globalisation of the Anglo-American approach to top-down, testbased educational accountability. In G.T.L. Brown & L.R. Harris (Eds.), *Handbook of human and social conditions in assessment* (pp. 387–403). New York: Routledge.

Lingard, B., Hayes, D., Mills, M., & Christie, P. (2003). *Leading learning: Making hope practical in schools*. Buckingham: Open University Press.

Povedano, A., Cava, M.J., Monreal, M.C., Varela, R., & Musitu, G. (2015). Victimization, loneliness, overt and relational violence at the school from a gender perspective. *International Journal of Clinical and Health Psychology, 15*(1), 44–51. https://doi.org/10.1016/j.ijchp.2014.09.001.

Povey, J., Campbell, A. K., Willis, L. D., Haynes, M., Western, M., Bennett, S., & Pedde, C. (2016). Engaging parents in schools and building parent-school partnerships: The role of school and parent organisation leadership. *International Journal of Educational Research, 79*, 128–141. https://doi.org/10.1016/j.ijchp.2014.09.001.

Putnam, R.D. (2001). Social capital: Measurement and consequences. In J.F. Helliwell (Eds.), *The contribution of human and social capital to sustained economic growth and well-being* (pp. 117–135). Ottawa, Ontario, Canada: Human Resources Development Canada.

Rawolle, S. (2010). Understanding the mediatisation of educational policy as practice. *Critical Studies in Education, 51*(1), 21–39. https://doi.org/10.1080/17508480903450208.

Rawolle, S., & Lingard, B. (2013). Bourdieu and educational research: Thinking tools, relational thinking, beyond epistemological innocence. In M. Murphy (Ed.), *Social theory and education research understanding Foucault, Habermas, Bourdieu and Derrida* (pp. 117–137). New York: Routledge.

Senge, P. M. (2012). Creating schools for the future, not the past for *all* students. *Leader to Leader, 65*, 44–49.

Shaked, H. (2018). Why principals sidestep instructional leadership: The disregarded question of schools' primary objective. *Journal of School Leadership, 28*(4), 517–538. https://doi.org/10.1177%2F105268461802800404.

Shaked, H., & Benoliel, P.S. (2020). Instructional boundary management: The complementarity of instructional leadership and boundary management. *Educational Management Administration & Leadership, 48*(5), 821–839. https://doi.org/10.1177%2F1741143219846905.

Shapira-Lishchinsky, O. (2018). *International aspects of organizational ethics in educational systems*. Emerald Group Publishing.

Skaalvik, E. M., & Skaalvik, S. (2017). Motivated for teaching? Associations with school goal structure, teacher self-efficacy, job satisfaction and emotional exhaustion. *Teaching and Teacher Education, 67*, 152–160. https://doi.org/10.1016/j.tate.2017.06.006.

Spillane, J. P., Halverson, R., & Diamond, J. B. (2001). Investigating school leadership practice: A distributed perspective. *Educational Researcher, 30*(3), 23–28.

Sun, J., & Leithwood, K. (2017). Calculating the power of alternative choices by school leaders for improving student achievement. *School Leadership & Management, 37*(1–2), 80–93. https://doi.org/10.1080/13632434.2017.1293635.

Theron, L. C. (2016). Toward a culturally and contextually sensitive understanding of resilience: Privileging the voices of black, South African young people. *Journal of Adolescent Research, 31*(6), 635–670. https://doi.org/10.1177%2F0743558415600072.

Thomson, P. (2001). How principals lose 'face': A disciplinary tale of educational administration and modern managerialism. *Discourse, 22*(1), 5–22. https://doi.org/10.1080/01596300120039722.

Thomson, P. (2010). Head teacher autonomy: A sketch of a Bourdieuian field analysis of position and practice. *Critical Studies in Education, 51*(1), 5–20. https://doi.org/10.1080/17508480903450190.
Tschannen-Moran, M. (2014). *Trust matters: Leadership for successful schools*. John Wiley & Sons.
Valli, L., Stefanski, A., & Jacobson, R. (2018). School-community partnership models: implications for leadership. *International Journal of Leadership in Education, 21*(1), 31–49. https://doi.org/10.1080/13603124.2015.1124925.
Valois, R. F., Kerr, J. C., & Huebner, S. E. (2012). Peer victimization and perceived life satisfaction among early adolescents in the United States. *American Journal of Health Education, 43*(5), 258–268. https://doi.org/10.1080/19325037.2012.10599244.
Varela, J. J., Zimmerman, M. A., Ryan, A. M., Stoddard, S. A., Heinze, J. E., & Alfaro, J. (2018). Life satisfaction, school satisfaction, and school violence: A mediation analysis for Chilean adolescent victims and perpetrators. *Child Indicators Research, 11*(2), 487–505. https://doi.org/10.1007/s12187-016-9442-7.
Wacquant, L. (1989). Corps et âme. *Actes de la recherche en sciences sociales, 80*(1), 33–67.
Wang, F. (2018). Social justice leadership—Theory and practice: A case of Ontario. *Educational Administration Quarterly, 54*(3), 470–498. https://doi.org/10.1177%2F0013161X18761341.
Weick, K. (2009). Enacting an environment: The infrastructure of organizing. In R. Westwood and S. Clegg (Eds.), *Debating organization: Point-counterpoint in organizational studies*. London: Blackwell.
Wrigley, T. (2003). *Schools of hope: A new agenda for school improvement*. Stoke on Trent, UK: Trentham Books.
Yablon, Y. B. (2019). School safety and school connectedness as resilience factors for students facing terror. *School Psychology, 34*(2), 129–137. https://psycnet.apa.org/doi/10.1037/spq0000259.
Yablon, Y. B., & Addington, L. A. (2018). Students' feeling of safety in Israeli schools: A place-based perspective. *Psychology of violence, 8*(4), 401–408. https://psycnet.apa.org/doi/10.1037/vio0000133.

Chapter Six

Leading the School Organization in the Evolving 21st-Century Legal Environment

R. Stewart Mayers

INTRODUCTION

Today's school leaders often deal with legal issues that, a generation ago, did not exist. Others existed, but for various reasons, rarely found a way into public discourse, not to mention courts of law. The reasons for the evolution of legal issues faced by school leaders include changing attitudes, new statutes, and new interpretations of existing statutes or clauses of the constitution. Additionally, technological advances also result in new legal challenges. While technology evolves daily, legal action can take months if not years to find its way into a court of law. These badly mismatched timelines exacerbate the already daunting challenges school leaders face in the 21st century.

Management can be defined as "the process of administering and controlling the affairs of the organization, irrespective of its nature, type, structure, and size" (Business Jargons, 2018, para 1). For school leaders in years past, "controlling" those affairs and activities seemed less formidable. Technology evolved at a much slower pace, meaning the gap between the pace at which new challenges arose and the speed at which courts of law provided guidance for managing those challenges was much smaller. In the 21st century, management by itself is insufficient. Today's schools need leaders who can anticipate challenges and can creatively use the guidance available to choose a direction, formulate policy, and identify solutions to address those challenges.

In this chapter, challenges specific to the 21st-century legal landscape in schools will be discussed. These include expanded interpretation of Title VII employment discrimination protection, technology-driven changes in speech and search law, as well as current issues in Title IX of the Education Amendments of 1972.

TITLE VII: EMPLOYMENT DISCRIMINATION

According to the National Center for Education Statistics, public schools in the United States spent 80% of their operating budgets on salaries and benefits for employees during the 2016–17 (the latest year for which statistics are available) school year (National Center for Education Statistics, 2020). Since employees play such a key role in the success of any organization, ensuring the fair and equitable selection of quality staff is paramount to the successful operation of schools. The consequences of non-compliance with employment law in general, and Title VII in particular, can be quite costly.

Title VII was passed as a part of the Civil Rights Act of 1964 in response to historical disparities in employment opportunities, particularly among racial groups. To afford equal employment opportunities across demographic groups, Title VII requires employers, including public schools, to base employment decisions on applicant qualifications and job duties alone. Since its passage, Title VII has been applied specifically to public schools in the areas of religion and retaliation.

Title VII and the Public Schools

In 1986, teacher Ronald Philbrook challenged a district policy that forbade him from using personal or sick leave to observe religious obligations. While the district provided three days of annual leave for religious purposes, its policy forbade employees from using additional personal leave for religious purposes. Reversing the trial court's opinion in favor of the board, the Supreme Court held, "unpaid leave is not a reasonable accommodation when paid leave is provided for all purposes except religious ones. A provision for paid leave 'that is part and parcel of the employment relationship may not be doled out in a discriminatory fashion, even if the employer would be free ... not to provide the benefit at all'" (*Ansonia Board of Education v. Philbrook*, 1986, p. 70–71).

The most recent Title VII cases involving public schools addressed the issue of retaliation. The 5th Circuit held the termination of a principal's secretary that was based partially on her filing of an EEOC complaint against the principal's predecessor, violated Title VII (*Fabela v. Socorro Independent School District*, 2003). A Florida appellate court held that a school violated Title VII's provisions against retaliation by refusing to allow a former employee who recently resigned from the district from continuing to serve as a volunteer mentor in the district (*Gates v. Gadsden County School Board*, 2010). Currently, the area of Title VII under the closest judicial scrutiny has surrounding sex.

Title VII and Sex

The final version of the law included the word "sex." This floor amendment, introduced by Representative Howard Worth Smith of Virginia, was introduced in the waning moments of debate, and left little legislative history to help clarify Representative Smith's intent. This ambiguity led some to believe Smith wanted to prevent the bill's passage, not to support women's rights in the workplace (Whalen & Whalen, 1985). The lack of clarity concerning Smith's motives led courts to originally interpret the word sex in Title VII narrowly.

One of the first court cases concerning the meaning of the word sex in Title VII occurred more than a decade following the law's passage (*Voyles v. Ralph K. Davies Medical Center*, 1975). In *Voyles*, Charles Volyes, a hemodialysis technician was terminated due to his intention to undergo sex reassignment surgery. The court concluded nowhere in case law nor in its legislative history does Title VII give any indication of an intent to provide protection based on transgender status. The Voyles court asserted, "Situations involving transsexuals, homosexuals, or bisexuals were simply not considered, and from this void the court is not permitted to fashion its own judicial interdictions" (*Volyes v. Davies*, p. 457).

This same narrow definition of sex dominated the federal court's interpretation of Title VII throughout the 1970s and 1980s (see *Powell v. Read's*, 1977; *Sommers v. Budget Marketing*, 1982; *Lyng v. Castillo*, 1986). Further reinforcement of the narrow definition of sex came from the 7th Circuit Court of Appeals in its opinion in *Ulane v. Eastern Airlines* (1984). Kenneth Ulane, a decorated army pilot from the Vietnam War, was hired by Eastern Airlines as a pilot. Eleven years after being hired, Ulane underwent psychiatric treatment. Later, Ulane had sex reassignment surgery and began using a new name, Karen Ulane. After being fired by Eastern, Ulane sued, claiming her termination violated Title VII.

The trial court judge asked the question that would perplex courts for years to come, "What did we get when we got sex?" (*Ulane v. Eastern Airlines*, 1983, p. 822). The trial court concluded sex was both a physical as well as a psychological issue and ordered Ulane's reinstatement. However, the 7th Circuit Court of Appeals reversed, believing a new, broader definition of sex should come from Congress and not the courts (*Ulane v. Eastern Airlines*, 1984). In 1989, the U.S. Supreme Court decided *Price Waterhouse v. Hopkins*, changing the landscape of Title VII case law.

In 1982, Ann Hopkins was proposed for partnership in the accounting firm of Price Waterhouse. Despite glowing reviews of her work, Hopkins's application for the partnership was put on hold for consideration the following year. Evidence in the case revealed the male partners believed Hopkins was not feminine enough. One partner suggested she "take a course at charm school" (*Price Waterhouse v. Hopkins,* 1989, p. 235). A plurality of the Court concluded that discrimination based on sexual stereotypes constituted discrimination based on sex. This shift in interpretation began a trend toward a broader definition of sex in Title VII litigation.

This new interpretation of Title VII was further expanded with the Supreme Court's decision in *Bostock v. Clayton County Board of Commissioners* (2020). In *Bostock,* the Court held Title VII did provide protection based on sexual orientation and sexual identity. The Court provided a caveat that, although other statutes may provide some protection to employers who discriminate based on sexual orientation or sexual identity based on sincerely held religious beliefs, how those other statutes that protect religious liberty "interact with Title VII are questions for future cases" (*Bostock v. Clayton County,* p. 32).

For public schools, it is incumbent on school leaders to be sure all who are involved in the hiring process, including teachers on interviewing committees are trained in the latest interpretation of Title VII protections. School leaders must also continuously monitor the school's climate to ensure all employees are respected and supported in the workplace.

SOCIAL MEDIA/TECHNOLOGY

Technology evolves constantly. Litigation is a slow process in which a dispute may take years to get to court and even longer to potential appeal in higher courts. The tension between these two disparate timelines means school leaders often make decisions with legal ramifications based on limited guidance from the courts. At times, this guidance takes the form of cases decided long before the technology at the heart of the dispute was even invented. Two fundamental rights that have often been the subject of these disputes are freedom of speech and the right to be free from unreasonable searches.

Free Speech

Few inventions have completely changed the landscape of communications like the smartphone. The landmark Supreme Court decisions that still control the analysis of speech claims by students and school employees were both decided in the 1960s. In *Tinker v. Des Moines Community School District* (1969), the Court upheld the constitutionality of public school students to wear black armbands with white peace symbols to school in protest of the Vietnam War. The Court concluded student speech in schools is protected under the first amendment unless, "students' activities would materially and substantially disrupt the work and discipline of the school" (*Tinker v. Des Moines*, 1969, p. 513). In its opinion, the Court asserted, "It can hardly be argued that either students or teachers shed their constitutional rights to freedom of speech or expression at the schoolhouse gate" (*Tinker v. Des Moines*, 1969, p. 507). The "schoolhouse gate" metaphor worked well in 1969. It is not as well suited for addressing disputes that can arise in 21st-century schools.

The introduction of smartphones has significantly complicated school leaders' decision-making about when a student's speech can or should be sanctioned. The capability of these devices has complicated the usage of the *Tinker* Court's schoolhouse gate metaphor in analyzing student speech claims. A prime example is the case of Taylor Bell (*Bell v. Itawamba County Board of Education* (2015). In 2011, while a student at an Itawamba County high school, Taylor Bell wrote, performed, and published (on Facebook and YouTube) a rap song in which he accused two coaches at his school of inappropriately touching female students. Included in the song's lyrics was a reference to wanting to "cap" the coaches. Bell and his mother filed suit in federal court (*Bell v. Itawamba County*, 2012).

The district court held that Bell's speech met the *Tinker* material and substantial disruption standard because Bell's speech "caused a material and/or substantial disruption at the school and that it was reasonably foreseeable to school officials the song would cause such a disruption" (*Bell v. Itawambe County*, 2012, p. 840). In response to his song, school officials decided to suspend Bell indefinitely pending a hearing. At the hearing, the school board's disciplinary committee concluded Bell's song constituted a threat against the coaches, suspended Bell for seven days, and then transferred him to an alternative educational placement for the remaining five weeks of the grading term.

A three-judge panel of the 5th Circuit Court of Appeals overturned the district court's decision. The panel concluded since Bell's song was recorded off-campus at a professional recording studio and that he used his home computer to post the song to the internet outside of school hours, Bell's speech was beyond school officials' ability to sanction. Further, the panel concluded school officials had failed to demonstrate that Bell's song "caused a substantial disruption of schoolwork or discipline, or that school officials reasonably could have forecast such a disruption" (*Bell v. Itawamba County*, 2014, p. 282). Itawamba County school officials requested and were granted an appeal to the en banc 5th Circuit.

In 2015, 16 active judges of the 5th Circuit Court of Appeals heard argument in Bell's case. In his argument before the en banc 5th Circuit, Bell argued that *Tinker* only applies to speech "inside the schoolhouse gate" (*Bell v. Itawamba County*, 2015, p. 392). In response, the court referred to the Supreme Court's holding in *Morse v. Frederick*, in which Justice Alito pointed out that, "when *Tinker* was decided, Internet, cellphones, smartphones and digital social media did not exist" (*Bell v. Itawamba County*, 2015, p. 392). The en banc court overturned the judgment of the three-judge panel, holding Bell's speech presented a foreseeable material and substantial disruption to the school.

The student cyber speech cases that have reached the federal courts fit into three major categories: bogus profiles, threats, and cyberbullying (Mayers, 2015). When students create bogus profiles of school officials, the courts have consistently held this speech, regardless of how vulgar, to be protected (see *Layshock v. Hermitage*, 2010 and *J.S. v. Blue Mountain School District*, 2011). In the case of threats and cyberbullying, the students involved have been decidedly less successful in court.

In *O.Z. v. Board of Trustees, Long Beach Unified School District* (2008), a federal district court concluded a slideshow posted on YouTube which depicted the murder of O.Z.'s English teacher was not protected speech. Similarly, instant messages sent from home in which a student discussed plans to get a gun and shoot classmates at his school were not found to be protected speech (*D.J.M. v. Hannibal Public Schools*, 2011). A MySpace page, created at home to cyberbully another student and which led to bullying behavior at school, was not protected speech according to the 8th Circuit Court of Appeals (*Kowalski v. Berkeley*, 2011). During 2021, the Supreme Court accepted its first student social media speech case involving a vulgar rant by an angry cheerleader sent from off campus. The Court applied the *Tinker* test and held that the school violated the cheerleader's free speech rights because there was no disruption to the school (Mahanoy Area School District v. B.L. 594 U.S. _____ 2021).

The year before *Tinker*, the Supreme Court decided *Pickering v. Board of Education* (1968), still the Court's landmark decision concerning employee speech. In *Pickering*, the Court held a high school teacher's letter to the editor of a local newspaper in which he criticized local school administrators' distribution of bond issue proceeds was protected speech. The Court reasoned that a teacher's speech, made as a private citizen, on matters of public concern, and that did not interfere with the teacher's duties or the operation of the school, was "entitled to the same protection as if they had been made by a member of the general public" (*Pickering v. Board*, p. 564). Social media has blurred the lines between speech as a private citizen and speech as a public employee.

As with student speech, technology has complicated decision-making for school leaders regarding managing the effects of employee speech in public schools. The courts continue to use the three-prong test from *Pickering* that the employee must (1) be speaking as a private individual (2) on a matter of public concern and (3) the speech cannot cause disruption in the operation of the school (*Pickering v. Board of Education*, 1968, pp. 563–564). While the courts agree that social media speech is private speech, complications arise when there is a mixture of speech which does address matters of public concern and speech that does not.

This issue was addressed in *Spanierman v. Hughes* (2008). In *Spanierman*, the court found a poem about war posted to a MySpace page to be a matter of public concern, and the remaining speech on the site was not. The two were analyzed separately. Consistently, courts adjudicating employee social media speech have relied on the 3rd prong of *Pickering*. Speech that is derogatory toward members of the school community (see *Munroe v. Central Bucks County Board of Education*, 2014) or that facilitates inappropriate interactions between employees and students (see *Spanierman v. Hughes*, 2008) are not protected under the first amendment.

Decision-making is a fundamental skill for leaders. Making appropriate decisions requires understanding the context surrounding the decision. Employee social media speech claims illustrate this principle. The *Munroe* court asserted, "Context is crucial, as the employing agency's institutional efficiency may be threatened not only by the content of the employee's message, but also by the manner, time, and place in which it is delivered" (p. 537).

In 2009, a Georgia teacher posted vacation pictures of herself on social media, one of which depicted her drinking a glass of wine. At the time, the district had a policy that indicated employees could "be investigated, disciplined and terminated for postings on websites that contain provocative photographs, sexually explicit messages, use of alcohol, drugs or anything students are not supposed to do" (Marshall, 2011, para 1). The photos were brought to the attention of school leaders in an anonymous email. School officials then pressured Ms. Payne to resign her job. Threats to suspend her from her job began less than two hours after receipt of the email (Downey, 2009).

Many questions could be asked about this situation. Did the administration take sufficient time to determine the context surrounding the posting of these photos? Did the posted photos truly demonstrate conduct that would make a teacher unfit for the classroom? According to Marshall (2011), the teacher had her account set to the most stringent privacy setting so students could not access the account or the picture that set off the controversy that made its way to the public when a "friend" of the teacher's shared the photo. Determining the context in which the photos were taken can provide school leaders more clarity about situations before making personnel decisions.

Searches and Technology

The prevalence of smartphones in schools has introduced another issue in schools, technology-related searches. Unlike cellular telephones of the past, smartphones are computers capable of storing much personal information. They are cameras, voice recorders, appointment calendars, and so more. The practice of sexting has introduced the issue of pornographic images (Mayers & Desiderio, 2013). Deciding when and if to search a student's smartphone is not always a clear decision. To date, three cases have been heard in federal court addressing cellphone searches. All three applied the reasonableness standard of *New Jersey v. TLO* (1985).

In *Klump v. Nazareth Area School District* (2006), the court held school officials using a student's cellphone to call other students in the phone's address book to determine which other students had cellphones with them, constituted an unreasonable search. Four years later, a federal district court concluded, although with some reservation, that school safety was more important than the student's privacy interests, therefore a search of student's photographs did not violate the 4th amendment's prohibition of unreasonable searches.

Finally, in *Mendoza v. Klein Independent School District* (2011), the court held the associate principal conducted two searches. The court found the first search (of the front page of the messaging app) reasonable because the student was observed typing a text during instructional hours. However, the court concluded the second search (of the student's photographs) was not reasonable. In the court's view, the associate principal did not have sufficient reasonable suspicion to support such an invasive search. The only clarity in this area of the law for school leaders is very limited guidance about cellphone searches from the courts.

Whether the issue is speech or search and seizure, public schools need to provide students and employees specific policies that provide guidance about the appropriate use of technology. These policies need to include boundaries for appropriate usage, protection for employee and student rights, and due process for resolving disputes. As with all policies, technology policies need to be reviewed periodically in light of advances in apps and devices and changes in the law.

TITLE IX

Perhaps the greatest legal challenge for 21st-century school leaders is Title IX. Enacted in 1972, Title IX provides:

> No person in the United States shall, on the basis of sex, be excluded from participation in, be denied the benefits of, or be subjected to discrimination under

any education program or activity receiving Federal financial assistance. (Title IX, 1972, p. 1)

Title IX requires equal opportunity in all services and programs offered by educational institutions. Initially, the main application of the law was to athletics. To comply, educational institutions added sports for women to their extracurricular offerings. Participation of male-to-female transgender students in athletics has caused controversy.

In Connecticut, Selina Soule, Alanna Smith, and Chelsea Mitchell, high school track athletes, filed suit against the Connecticut Association of Schools claiming the Association violated their rights under Title IX by allowing a transgender girl to participate in interscholastic track meets. Further, the plaintiffs claimed injury in the form of a loss of scholarship opportunities. The court held that Soule's case was moot since the plaintiffs had graduated; an appeal is now before the Second Circuit in New York City.

On March 11, 2021, Governor Tate Reeves of Mississippi signed into law, Senate Bill 2536 which bans transgender girls from participating on girls' sports teams. (Reuters, 2021). As of March 2021, 35 bills have been introduced to ban transgender students from participating on teams based on their sexual identity (Wilson, 2021).

In some cases, litigation involves transgender students who have no affiliation with sports teams. These cases often deal with bathroom usage, implicating privacy rights. To date, the federal courts have provided little guidance for school leaders to formula and implement policy in their schools. Four federal court cases have addressed the issue of transgender students and restroom usage. These cases are constrained within three circuits. Two of these occurred in the territory of the 7th Circuit Court of Appeals (*Whitaker v. Kenosha*, 2017; *Students and Parents for Privacy v. United States Department of Education*, 2016) one from the 6th Circuit (*Dodds v. United States Department of Education*, 2016), and the 4th Circuit (*Grimm v. Gloucester County Board of Education*, 2020).

While each of these courts above held that allowing transgender students to use bathrooms consistent with their sexual identity did not violate Title IX, these cases are only applicable to 12 states. One case addressed this issue in the context of higher education (*Johnson v. University of Pittsburgh*, 2015). The *Johnson* court concluded that prohibiting transgender students from using restroom and locker room facilities consistent with their sexual identity did not violate Title IX.

The challenges of serving transgender students are exacerbated by Congress leaving specifics about the implementation of Title IX to the executive branch. This places important policy with little stability due to the different points of view concerning transgender rights by various administrations. In

2016, the Obama administration issued a "Dear Colleague" letter to provide guidance for school leaders in the area of Title IX compliance. In part, this document asserted that:

> The Departments treat a student's gender identity as the student's sex for purposes of Title IX and its implementing regulations. This means that a school must not treat a transgender student differently from the way it treats other students of the same gender identity. (Department of Justice and Department of Education, 2016, p. 2)

In 2017, the Trump administration issued its own "Dear Colleague" letter. This letter withdrew in its entirety, the May 2016 Dear Colleague letter. According to the Trump Dear Colleague letter, the Obama Administration letter did not "contain extensive legal analysis or explain how the position is consistent with the express language of Title IX, nor did they undergo any formal public process" (Department of Justice and Department of Education, 2017, p. 1).

On his first day in office, President Joe Biden issued his "Executive Order on Preventing and Combating Discrimination on the Basis of Gender Identity or Sexual Orientation" (2021) which countermanded the Dear Colleague from the Trump administration. Sadly, the people's representatives in Congress have been either unable or unwilling to fashion a long-term solution to Title IX interpretation that would provide more stability in this law.

As with technology, policies and procedures relative to Title IX need to be reviewed periodically, particularly in light of the changing position of the executive branch of the federal government. Those who are charged with the investigation of or due process for Title IX claims need to be trained and to have the training updated regularly. Without guidance from the Supreme Court, public schools need expert advice from legal counsel that is up to date.

CONCLUSION

In their groundbreaking work, *A Leadership Guide to Navigating the Unknown*, Zepeda and Lanoue (2021), discuss "pivoting decisions rapidly" and "shifting traditional systems" (p. 149). They explain:

> System leaders continued to grapple with what may be the most difficult decisions of their careers: how to best structure learning conditions that could keep students, staff, and community members safe amid the unknowns.... Opposing positions from internal and external stakeholders ... placed leaders in no-win situations. (p. 149)

The 21st-century legal landscape echoes with these same concerns about protecting the safety of school community members.

Since the Supreme Court's decision in *Bostock*, questions about the implementation of Title VII protections seem settled. However, the Supreme Court has yet to weigh in on Title IX's commands about the transgender community. Dear Colleague letters and the sparse number of lower court decisions have failed to provide consistent, stable guidance for school leaders. To complicate the situation further, Congress has failed to provide guidance for school leaders as well.

Leading schools in the evolving 21st-century legal environment will continue to challenge school leaders. The costs of involvement in the legal system are varied and costly. Disputes between a school and its stakeholders can damage relationships. Schools require healthy relationships with students, parents, and others for learning to occur. Legal disputes can damage relationships, at times beyond repair. Litigation is also costly in terms of time. In 2015, the average length of civil litigation was 8.7 months. By 2017, that number rose to 10.4 months. Often, politics that leave judgeships vacant are part of the problem by creating a backlog of cases to be heard. Civil litigation can last several years (Biggs, 2018). The human cost to a school district is significant with depositions, document production, and meetings with legal counsel.

Finally, the financial cost is considerable. There are the obvious costs of attorneys, mediators, document production, investigator fees, and arbitrators, to name a few. However, there are also hidden costs. These include loss of employee productivity and employee stress. Coupled with the extended time normally involved in civil litigation, these costs are considerable, to the individual employee and to the school.

Protecting the school from the myriad costs of entanglement in the legal system requires a premeditated plan of action. School leaders need adequate professional development to prepare them with the tools for managing incidents that implicate the legal system. These skills include proper planning for specific situations and having appropriate policies in place to support the school's preparation to deal with these situations. School leaders also need a basic knowledge of the law and the legal system to react appropriately, advise other employees on their actions, and provide needed information and artifacts to the district's legal counsel.

All school districts need quality legal counsel to provide the advice necessary to navigate the tricky waters presented by legal issues in schools. School leaders, particularly the superintendent, need a strong working relationship with the board's attorney. Accurate, timely communication is essential when addressing legal issues in schools.

School leaders need to ensure continuous professional development for all employees. Because the landscape of education law is always evolving, professional development must also evolve so employees' knowledge is up to date. Having staff properly trained can be a proactive way of avoiding liability. Fewer employees will likely, through their conduct, place schools in a situation where legal liability can occur. Also, proactive school leaders can remove a lack of training as a basis for a claim in court.

The law exists to protect the rights of citizens to participate fully in society and to provide access to educational opportunities. The law also exists to help ensure equitable and consistent outcomes when disputes end up in court. School leaders of the 21st century need to continuously prepare themselves and their schools for success in navigating the ever-evolving landscape of education law.

CASE STUDY

Dr. Jerry Larson is the high school principal in a small, rural community. A new family that has just moved to town has informed him their transgender daughter who just enrolled, will be joining the school's softball team and fully expects to use the same locker room and restroom facilities as the other players. The families of several girls who are key players on the team are highly influential families in the community. They have denounced the idea of a biologically male student in their daughters' locker room and restroom. Simply put, they are offended by the idea of this new student just being on the team. Members of the community are deeply upset, as evidenced by the tension at a recent board meeting. Three of the five members of the school board have publicly announced their adamant opposition to allowing a transgender girl on the softball team.

Dr. Larson asked for a meeting with the superintendent, Dr. Linda Van. At that meeting, Dr. Van told Dr. Larson she agrees with the board majority to not allow the new student on the softball team. Further, you asked for permission to speak with the board's attorney, a request that was denied. Based on the information presented in this chapter and your research, what should Dr. Larson do? What should he tell the new family? The girls on the team?

REFERENCES

Ansonia Board of Education v. Philbrook, 479 U.S. 60.
Bell v. Itawamba County School Board, 859 F.Supp. 2d 834 (N.D. Miss. 2012).
Bell v. Itawamba County School Board, 774 F.3d 280 (5th Cir. 2014).

Bell v. Itawamba County School Board, 799 F.3d 379 (5th Cir. 2015).
Biggs, A. (2018). Lack of judges leads to longer litigation times. https://www.pilieromazza.com/lack-of-judges-leads-to-longer-litigation-times/.
Bostock v. Clayton County Board of Commissioners 590 U.S. (2020).
Business Jargons (2018). Management. Business Jargons. https://businessjargons.com/management.html.
Civil Rights Act of 1964, 42 U.S.C §§ 2000e-1 et seq (1964).
D.J.M. v. Hannibal Public Sch. Dist., 647 F.3d 754 (8th Cir. 2011).
Department of Justice and Department of Education (2016). Dear colleague letter (May 13, 2016). https://www2.ed.gov/about/offices/list/ocr/letters/colleague-201605-title-ix-transgender.pdf.
Department of Justice and Department of Education (2017). Dear colleague letter (February 22, 2017). https://www2.ed.gov/about/offices/list/ocr/letters/colleague-201702-title-ix.pdf.
Dodds v. United States Dept. of Educ., 845 F.3d 217 (6th Cir. 2016).
Downey, M. (2009). Barrow teacher done in by anonymous "parent" email about her Facebook page. http://blogs.ajc.com/get-schooled-blog/2009/11/13/barrow-teacher-done-in-by-anonymous-e-mail-withperfect-punctuation/.
Executive Order (2021). Executive order on preventing and combating discrimination on the basis of gender identity or sexual orientation. https://www.whitehouse.gov/briefing-room/presidential-actions/2021/01/20/executive-order-preventing-and-combating-discrimination-on-basis-of-gender-identity-or-sexual orientation/.
Fabela v. Socorro Independent School District, 329 F.3d 409 (5th Cir. 2003).
Gates v. Gadsden County School Board, 45 So.3d 39, District Court of Appeal of Florida, First District (2010).
Grimm v. Gloucester County Board of Education, No. 19-1952 (4th Cir. 2020).
J.S. v. Blue Mountain School District, 650 F.3d 915 (3d Cir. 2011).
Johnson v. University of Pittsburgh, 97 F.Supp. 3d 657 (W.D. Pa., 2015).
Klump v. Nazareth Area School District, 425 F.Supp.2d 622 (E.D. Pa. 2006).
Kowalski v. Berkeley Cnty. Sch., 652 F.3d 565 (4th Cir. 2011).
Layshock v. Hermitage School District, 593 F.3d 249 (3rd Cir. 2010).
Lyng v. Castillo, 477 U.S. 635 (1986).
Mahanoy Area School District v. B.L. 594 U.S. _____ (2021).
Marshall, J. (2011). The Ashley Payne affair revisited. https://ethicsalarms.com/2011/02/08/the-ashley-payne-affair-revisited/.
Mayers, R.S. (2015). *Social media, public schools, and the law*. Education Law Association.
Mayers, R.S., & Desiderio, M.F. (2013). Legal issues encountered during one high school's response to sexting. *Brigham Young Education and Law Journal, 2013*(1), 1–20.
Mendoza v. Klein Indep. Sch. Dist. H-09-3895. (S.D. Tex. 2011).
Munroe v. Central Bucks Sch. Dist, I, 34 F.Supp.3d 532 (E.D. Pa 2014).
National Center for Education Statistics (2020). Table 236.20. Total expenditures for public elementary and secondary education and other related programs, by function

and sub-function: Selected years, 1990–91 through 2016–17. https://nces.ed.gov/programs/digest/d19/tables/dt19_236.20.asp.

New Jersey v. T. L. O., 469 U.S. 325 (1985).

O.Z. v. Bd. of Trustees of the Long Beach Unified Sch. Dist., CV 08-5671 ODW (AJWx) (C.D. CA 2008).

Pickering v. Board of Education, 391 U.S. 563 (1968).

Powell v. Read's, Inc., 436 F. Supp. 369 (D. Md. 1977).

Price Waterhouse v. Hopkins, 490 U.S. 228 (1989).

Reuters (2021). Mississippi governor signs law banning transgender athletes in women's sport. https://www.reuters.com/article/us-usa-lgbtq-sports-mississippi/mississippi-governor-signs-law-banning-transgender-athletes-from-womens-sports-idU.S.KBN2B32HV.

Sommers v. Budget Marketing, Inc., 667 F.2d 748 (8th Cir. 1982).

Soule v. Connecticut Association of Schools, Inc. (2020). Verified complaint for declaratory and injunctive relief and damages.

Spanierman v. Hughes, 576 F.Supp.2d 292 (D. Ct. 2008).

Students and Parents for Privacy v. United States Dept. of Educ. Case No. 16-cv-4945 (N.D. Ill. 2016)

Tinker v. Des Moines School Dist., 393 U.S. 503 (1969).

Title IX of the Education Amendments of 1972, 20 U.S.C. §§ 1681—1688.

Ulane v. Eastern Airlines, Inc., 581 F. Supp. 821 (N.D. Ill. 1983).

Ulane v. Eastern Airlines, Inc., 742 F.2d 1081 (7th Cir. 1984).

Voyles v. Ralph K. Davies Medical Center, 403 F.Supp. 456 (N.D. Cal. 1975).

Whalen, C., and Whalen, B. (1985). *The longest debate: A legislative history of the 1964 Civil Rights Act.* Seven Locks Press.

Whitaker v. Kenosha Unified Sch. Dist., 858 F.3d 1034 (7th Cir. 2017).

Wilson, R. (2021). Majority of states considering bills limiting transgender access. https://thehill.com/homenews/state-watch/541322-majority-of-states-considering-bills-limiting-transgender-access.

Zepeda, S.J., & Lanoue, P.D. (2021). *A leadership guide to navigating the unknown: New narratives amid COVID-19.* Routledge.

Chapter Seven

Leadership for Flourishing

Positive Approaches to Relationship Building

Benjamin Kutsyuruba

INTRODUCTION

Increasingly, research in education emphasizes the imperative of teaching, leading, organizing, and managing schools in ways that consider health, vibrancy, happiness, flourishing, and well-being as important indicators of student and school achievement (Hayward et al., 2007; Kim, 2016; Roffey, 2008; Tschannen-Moran & Clement, 2018). However, healthy and flourishing school organizations that promote students' well-being and thriving can only be developed if adults within them also experience well-being (Louis & Murphy, 2018).

From an ecological perspective, schools are viewed as living and breathing systems (Clarke, 2000; Wheatley, 1999), with emphasis on connectedness, contextual interdependency, and symbiotic relationships wherein difficult times for some will implicate challenges for others, and the celebrations of some or one will have ramifications on the lives of others (Walker et al., 2021). There are direct and indirect benefits of paying attention to the ecology of well-being and viewing schools as living systems, characterized by noticing and responding to challenges and issues within them from a positive, generative, and appreciative approach (Cooperrider, 2013; Roffey, 2008). Thus, asset-based adult relationships are a precondition for creating student well-being—only when all or most of the members of the school are thriving would educational institutions be able to make a positive contribution to the larger society (Louis & Murphy, 2018).

Critical in this regard is a positive, strength-based approach to school leadership that illuminates the opportunities and potentials for school improvement and creates conditions for others in school to flourish as a collective (Walker et al., 2021). Positive leadership goes beyond the traditional administration and management foci of school improvement and effectiveness, moving the leadership discourse and practice toward growing conditions for well-being and healthfulness, wholeness and vitality, thriving and flourishing. Louis and Murphy (2018) called this a spillover effect of positive organizational leadership: "because schools are socializing and preparing the next generation of citizens, positive outcomes at all levels will deepen socio-emotional learning for students and model positive adult work settings" (p. 166). Considering the important influence of school principals in transforming schools (Leithwood et al., 2010), studying school leadership through the lens of flourishing (Cherkowski et al., 2020; Cherkowski & Walker, 2013) can provide new insights for organizing schools for sustainable improvement, and has immediate consequences and implications for school management.

This chapter describes findings from a research study that examined perceptions of flourishing in the work lives of national award-winning principals in the Canada's Outstanding Principals (COP) program. This award recognizes outstanding contributions of principals in publicly funded schools who "demonstrate innovation and entrepreneurial spirit, and who have done something truly remarkable in public education" (The Learning Partnership, 2019). The research purpose was to examine how these outstanding principals experienced the sense of flourishing and what factors, in their opinion, contributed to working environments in schools where flourishing was possible and sustainable. This chapter provides a brief review of relevant literature and research methodology, describes participants' perceptions regarding the role of positive relationships for flourishing in schools, and offers implications for practice.

THEORETICAL FRAMEWORK

Theoretically, this study draws on the literature from the generative fields of positive psychology and positive organizational scholarship (Carr, 2004; Roberts & Dutton, 2009; Seligman et al., 2005). Scholars in these areas have highlighted the conditions, strengths, and virtues that enable individuals to thrive with a predominant focus on emotional well-being, measuring constructs such as happiness and optimism, as well as the antecedents, benefits, and consequences of positive emotions and feeling good (Keyes & Annas, 2009; Seligman et al., 2009). Focus on positive attitudes, capacities, and relationships in organizations has been found to increase resilience, vitality, engagement, and happiness, to decrease stress, anxiety, and depression, and to promote general well-being (Bakker & Schaufeli, 2008; Harter et al., 2003; Sin & Lyubomirsky, 2009). Well-being, as a balance point between an individual's resource pool and the challenges faced (Dodge et al., 2012), in turn has been associated with success and other positive outcomes (Lyubomirsky et al., 2005). In shifting the attention away from the deficit-based towards asset- or strength-based models of thinking, positive organizational studies demonstrated that positive leadership for flourishing has transformative impact on the workplace culture (Cameron, 2012; Dutton and Spreitzer, 2014; Quinn & Quinn, 2015).

Flourishing is a multi-layered and complex experience that resonates from within individual, interpersonal, and organizational perspectives. Individually, flourishing is a trait understood as the pinnacle of human functioning, characterized by goodness and wholeness, and is experienced on a continuum (Fredrickson & Losada, 2005; Gable & Haidt, 2005; Seligman, 2011). Those who flourish experience the opposite of languishing, a feeling that is characterized by the absence of mental health, yearning for more, or feeling stuck in a rut (Keyes, 2002, 2003). Flourishing individuals are more resilient and come closer to self-fulfillment, contentment, and happiness (Haybron, 2008; Martin & Marsh, 2006). Keyes (2016) described flourishing as "the achievement of a balanced life in which individuals feel good about lives in which they are functioning well" (p. 101).

Yet, flourishing is more than just pursuing inner happiness (emotional well-being); it also concerns positive positioning of oneself towards life (psychological well-being) and in relation to other individuals (social well-being). Whereas "self-acceptance, positive relations with others, personal growth, purpose in life, environmental mastery, and autonomy" signify positive psychological functioning, "social coherence, social actualization, social integration, social acceptance, and social contribution" represent aspects of positive social functioning (Keyes, 2002, pp. 108–109).

Flourishing, as Seligman (2011) argued, is experienced through five pillars of well-being: positive emotions, engagement, positive relationships, meaning and accomplishments (also known as PERMA model). He posited that collective manifestations of these pillars will result in feeling good and living well. Moreover, individuals can grow their sense of flourishing by paying attention to how they experience the five pillars, building opportunities for themselves to experience all of the pillars as often as possible, and learning to appreciate these opportunities while acknowledging that this desired goal of flourishing will be a constantly moving target. Another model, PROSPER, was proposed by Noble and McGrath (2015); it stands for Positivity, Relationships, Outcomes, Strengths, Purpose, Engagement, and Resilience. In both of these models, positive approach to relationships building has been noted as an important factor for promoting flourishing of all and improving organizations as enabling institutions.

Roffey (2012) argued that positive school relationships can make a significant difference on many levels, in many areas, and to all stakeholders. However, she continued, the most powerful influence on relational quality in a school is found with the school leader and the leadership team. School leaders' vision for the school and their ability to both communicate it effectively to others and also inspire their endorsement is fundamental to positive change (Roffey, 2007). Flourishing in school leadership consists of "creating conditions for teachers, students and others in the school to work together towards shared goals in climates of care, connection, trust, innovation and improvement, fun and laughter" (Cherkowski & Walker, 2016, p. 385). In order to foster positive relationships with teachers, students, and parents, and thus create flourishing school climates (Cherkowski et al., 2018; Cherkowski & Walker, 2013), school leaders must first be able to create these conditions for themselves.

METHODOLOGY

The exploratory mixed-methods research study of Canada's Outstanding Principals entailed several data collection phases in 2019. For the first phase, an online survey was constructed by the researchers based on the prior-completed systematic review of the literature and adaptations of related survey instruments (Bakker, 2008; Duckworth et al., 2007; Patterson et al., 2009; Spreitzer et al., 2005). In collaboration with the Learning Partnership, an organization that administers the program, all past recipients of the Canada's Outstanding Principals award were invited to provide their responses to 62 closed and 12 open-ended questions grouped into the following categories: flow, flourishing and thriving, resilience, grit, and well-being (for more information on survey findings, see Kutsyuruba et al., 2021). In total, 73 principals completed the surveys.

The majority of respondents (56%) indicated they have 21 to 30 years of experience as an educator, 37% indicated that they have 16 or more years of experience as a principal, and only 8% indicated having 5 years or less. As a follow-up to the survey, respondents were invited to participate in the second phase of data collection, telephone interviews. In total, semi-structured interviews were conducted with 20 COP awardees from the survey sample, lasting on average for 30 minutes and providing rich descriptive data.

This chapter draws on the qualitative data obtained through both the open-ended survey questions and the interviews. For open-ended survey questions, qualitative analysis was conducted using a mix of a priori and open coding through appropriate codes from the literature. The codes gathered from the participants responses were then grouped into themes. Subsequently, interview data were analyzed both deductively and inductively following standard coding processes for etic and emic approaches to data analysis (Creswell, 2014). Both etic and emic codes were then combined into categories, and categories into patterns or concepts. Comparison of thematic analyses from both research phases demonstrated significant importance assigned by the participants to the role of positive relationships building for flourishing in schools, which is detailed in this chapter.

RESEARCH FINDINGS

The findings from thematic analyses of survey responses and interviews demonstrated the reciprocal or mirroring nature of flourishing. When we inquired about what flourishing meant to the outstanding principals and how they experienced it on a daily basis, most of them tied their experiences of flourishing with that of the teachers and students. As one participant put it: "We are the mirrors that reflect the needs and challenges and accomplishments of our communities. We are the brand that sells the school. We are the walking advertisement that champions everyone in the building." Principals used metaphors of a "ripple effect" or "domino effect," noting that flourishing manifests itself as a cycle—whereby a flourishing principal leads to flourishing teachers, which leads to flourishing students, which in turn leads to a flourishing principal. They noted a reciprocal exchange between the flourishing of others and their flourishing, thus suggesting that the flourishing of one may be a precondition for the flourishing of another. One leader stressed the importance of relationships for flourishing:

> I'm going to keep coming back to the relationship piece because there's reciprocity in every relationship. It's also reciprocity when in a flourishing school community or certainly when "I'm flourishing," you can see people, stakeholders being equally engaged, equally enthusiastic, equally willing to have conversations. On my best day, other people, even if they're having a bad day, you can see that they rise to the standard, the modeling that they're seeing in me as a principal. There's also the opposite because you could come to work and have things going on in life, where the reciprocity is from another stakeholder who is flourishing, elevating certainly at my level. . . . It's a circular relationship, whereby demonstrating on a daily basis a genuine interest and time for any other stakeholder that it is often reciprocated as well.

Another principal with over fifteen years of experiences explained the connection of flourishing of the various stakeholders and herself as absolutely integral: "If I'm not flourishing, I'm not passing any of that trust in others, and I'm not providing them with the skills, and the values, and guiding them towards a shared purpose." Yet another leader noted, "I think the connection is very, very close because if the school is flourishing, then you see yourself as flourishing. I really do believe that a good principal makes a good school. You know that you're being effective when your teachers are being effective."

The outstanding school principals did not only observe a clear and strong connection between their flourishing and that of others in school, they were also interested in taking active leadership roles to ensure that their staff and students flourished. In this sense, flourishing in school encapsulated the success, health, and general happiness of the students, as well as the professional development and wellness of the teachers. For participants, a sense of flourishing appeared to feed on their ability to enforce a positive impact as school leaders by helping students grow and succeed, teachers to inspire and lead, and the school to meet and exceed goals and expectations.

Many participants viewed the connection between flourishing principals and teachers and students as a reflection of their impact as leaders. When role-modelled and nurtured by the school leaders, the impact of flourishing was evident for the participants in how it permeated the climate and culture in the school and fostered relationships characterized by trust, balance, and holistic health. In the words of one principal, a flourishing school is an indicator of healthy leadership: "I think if I'm flourishing it trickles down. I think that all these thoughts about the atmosphere of the school, or the culture of the school, or the health of the relationships in the school, are truly reflective of healthiness at the top."

For many, this healthiness was associated with thriving, that combined vitality (feeling alive, energized, and positive), having a sense of purpose, and cultivating positive and constructive relationships with others. Principals noted that they thrived when they experienced positive relationships and community. As one leader passionately shared, "I thrive when I have a deep sense of fulfilment; I feel connected to my students, staff, parents; I have confidence in my ability to achieve the school goals and strengthening relationships while doing so."

Other comments referred to thriving examples of when all professionals in the school modeled for students what positive relationships looked like in the school and there was plenty of healthy relationship building time. For one participant, vitality occurs when "the children and adults are happy and engaged in learning. You see evidence of positive relationships and learners who are meaningfully engaged." Many of the principals explained that positive relationships between the different players within the school were essential for the leaders' flourishing as well as the flourishing of a school as a whole.

Positive relationships building was seen as a multifaceted interpersonal concept due to the nature of the principals' role that required them to interact with a variety of people. As one principal argued, it is pivotal for the leaders' flourishing to:

> have a deep, deep personal and professional commitment to establishing relationships with each and every stakeholder as equal as possible. Certainly, getting to know the students, getting to know all staff, certainly getting to know families, community partners, and do it as much as possible. I think once good relationships are really established, then you're better able to know the people and help them stay healthy, well, flourishing. But it's this constant daily commitment to, first, fostering, then enhancing relationships with all people, and really modeling that behavior, and opening opportunities to cross-referenced relationships.

The multi-directionality of interactions required outstanding principals to establish and foster meaningful relationships at various inter-role and interpersonal levels.

Firstly, as several principals noted, in order for them to flourish it was important to maintain strong connections with individuals at the school board level. In the words of one participant, "what's essential [for flourishing] would be to have support from your superintendent and your board." For another principal, having positive relationships with superiors allowed her to feel trusted and be more creative: "I'm really blessed to have "bosses" that I can go to, who have been supportive, who have let me vent, but also let me be creative."

Secondly, many of the principals highlighted the importance of having a network of fellow principals that they can connect with to ask questions and share their experiences. As some of the principals explained, building relationships at this level helped make their role feel less isolating. Of particular importance for some was having a mentorship relationship in order to learn from an experienced administrator and to have someone to talk to. Additionally, some highlighted the benefits of working together and relying on vice-principals in their school buildings. One leader said: "I have two VPs with me, and we're always working together as well as the chaplain, and we'll always work together."

The third level of relationship building happened with the staff in their school. Principals expressed that to flourish in their role as school leader, they needed to build strong, positive, and trusting relationships with their staff members so as to have their support. One experienced school principal claimed, "[the] school is much more fun, if you got people all working together, going in the same direction, realizing projects, realizing successes, academic, performing, music, dance, you name it." Showing appreciation, expressing gratitude, and encouraging others were noted as effective strategies to build relationships with teachers. As one leader commented: "We will write a little note to staff when we see something that we're thankful for, or when we see someone is languishing a bit and they need a little note of encouragement." A further look at the data revealed that increasing the capacity of staff may also be linked to utilizing evidence-based methods, empowering, viewing the school as a small community, much like a family, and models of engagement and team building.

Fourthly, many of the principals emphasized that it was important to remain student-focussed and building capacity in students through positive relationships. A principal said, "We have a lot of students with anxiety and whatnot in school, so we're really focusing on resiliency and mindfulness—a positive mindset. We're getting trained in that area and then we're putting that to the kids having more self-sufficient in terms of how they get themselves through their own problems instead of having other people solve the problems for them." For another administrator, flourishing entailed first modeling for students and then helping them build their own constructive relationships that lead to mutual growth:

> For example, a student wants to talk about arts, finding another student who might have that equal passion, interest, and really, really connecting folks that are not only flourishing, and by connecting folks that are flourishing, they feed positively off of each other, and really create that real community of flourishing.

The last level of relationship building happened between the school and the community. Many principals explained that when they were able to connect and work closely with the broader community, they were able to flourish in their role. One of the principals stated:

> We're not just a school, we are visible in the community, so we're on mission half the time. We're doing things for the community; we're maintaining those connections in positive ways. We're bringing outside people in to talk with the kids. It's not just a factory where we put the kids through. And so, those positive relations with anybody and everybody outside the school helps maintain those connections for the kids, so that they can see what their role is going to be in their futures as we turn them into those global citizens that they are supposed to become.

In sum, as another leader noted, leaders have a relational imperative to "establish the culture of care, where no one is left out, and everybody is included." Findings showed that the leaders' deliberate focus on building positive relationships at various levels contributed to a positive school culture and climate.

DISCUSSION

This study's findings indicated that flourishing for Canada's outstanding principals was related to an ecological metaphor of reciprocal or circular cycle of flourishing, whereas if leaders saw others around them flourish, then they experienced it as well; on the contrary, they did not flourish if the others were not flourishing. Flourishing of school leaders is a vital pre-requisite of a flourishing school climate, because leaders share the responsibility of creating positive environments that promote personal growth of others (Leithwood & McAdie, 2007). In this sense, leaders hold the key to a positive school environment where students, teachers, and staff can experience well-being and flourish (Roffey, 2008). However, for principals to be able to support others in experiencing and developing these capacities, they themselves need to experience and develop them first (Dutton et al., 2006).

When school leaders flourish, then teachers, staff, and students are able to achieve their fullest potential and flourish as well. Research shows that fostering flourishing in the school community requires leaders who are themselves true examples and the embodiment of flourishing, those who can first show, then support flourishing in schools embody the positive including a flourishing leader (Cherkowski et al., 2020). The "ripple effect" or "domino effect" of flourishing they described, aligns with the phenomenon of positive social contagion (Cameron et al., 2011; Wilderom, 2011), where one's flourishing causes or leads to others' flourishing, creating an upward spiral (Fredrickson et al., 2021; Sekerka et al., 2011). Relationally rich positive practices, with positive emotions underlying the interactions between members, enable the social and emotional contagion that promoting flourishing of all in an organization (Cameron et al., 2011).

Flourishing has more to do with other people than it does with the person (Nelson et al., 2016). Research shows that positive relationships play a key role in flourishing not only in the workplace (Colbert et al., 2016), but also spill over into life in general (VanderWeele et al., 2019). Flourishing principals tend to focus on relational values and practices as a central platform of their vision for their schools and model positive relationships among school members. As Barth (2006) argued, the relationships among the educators in a school define all relationships within the school's culture; teachers and school leaders have the capacity to either enrich the culture through vigorously healthy or diminish the culture through dangerously competitive relationships. The value of building positive and strong relationships at multiple levels—central office administrators, other principals, staff, teachers, and students—echoed throughout the participants' narratives of flourishing. Positive emotions have a significant impact on positive relationships at work, as people are drawn to those who are happier and more optimistic (Langley, 2012).

Building positive relationships is considered as one of the four strategies for positive leadership behaviour, along with creating positive climate, establishing positive communication, and fostering positive meaning (Cameron, 2012). Findings from this study demonstrated that Canada's outstanding principals' relationship-building efforts directly benefited the overall climate, interactions, and creating purposeful and meaningful learning and working experience. Purpose is one of the positive values that can help school leaders promote a sense of flourishing at work for themselves and foster, encourage, and support conditions for flourishing for others (Cherkowski et al., 2020). Positive relationships allow leaders to tap into physiological, psychological, and emotional well-being of individuals, increase their health, safety, and security, and in turn improve the overall performance in the organization.

According to Cameron (2012), there are two main enablers of positive relationships in organizations—fostering positive energy and capitalizing on people's strengths. Our findings have pointed out that having positive, trusting, and collaborative relationships; feeling energized, motivated, and fulfilled; and staying focused and purposeful appeared to facilitate a sense of vitality in participating principals. Moreover, school leaders built positive energy in others by expressing gratitude, showing appreciation, and encouraging others in their schools. These findings support research claims that positive leaders serve as role models in the workplace by fostering positive energy, paying attention to people's positive attributes, and focusing on people's strengths (Carr, 2004; Scarnati, 2002).

CONCLUSIONS AND IMPLICATIONS FOR POSITIVE RELATIONSHIP BUILDING

This study's findings demonstrated the deep entanglement of the principals' flourishing with that of others through the relational aspects of their work lives. Flourishing in schools, as living ecosystems, is a cyclical phenomenon based on the relational interdependence and a combination of intrapersonal and interpersonal factors (Keyes, 2016). Moreover, positive leadership practices were shown to have positive impacts not only on the leaders' sense of flourishing and the school's collective sense of flourishing. By deliberately focusing on positive aspects of organizational life in managing schools, leaders can help achieve aspired levels of growth, peace, and prosperity across communities (Kim, 2016).

Therefore, this study supports the claim that it makes sense for all schools to focus on the ecological development of relational quality school-wide, for both educational excellence and authentic flourishing of all (Roffey, 2012). Trust is at the heart of positive leadership; it is a life-giving and energy boosting ingredient in living systems (Kutsyuruba & Walker, 2021). By fostering trust, positive leaders create resilient cultures by creating positive networks within their organizations and focusing on developing their employees' strengths (Mishra & Mishra, 2013). Through strategies that build positive relationships with multiple stakeholders in schools, principals can create positive work climates, improve communication, create purpose and meaning, and achieve extraordinary performance in school organizations (Cameron, 2012).

Since relationships seem to be the most influential facet of school principals' flourishing, the utter transformation of how principals interact with and draw energy from people could be a hidden yet strong contributor to addressing languishing and negative interactions in schools. Furthermore, if school leaders are critical role models for flourishing of the whole school, then finding the appropriate ways to effectively support the principals' work should be a priority. In this regard, school systems and policymakers should consider the price to be paid when the principals are not flourishing.

CASE STUDY

Bernard Davies is the new principal in Cassidy High School in an urban school with 2,500 students. The school has had three principals within a span of 5 years. The school, in short, is anything but "flourishing." There's faculty discontent, largely due to a lack of emotional and administrative support by the school administration. Teachers feel disrespected and say they are not treated as professionals. Parents have complained that curriculum standards are lacking, and they are dissatisfied with the general level of student achievement based on standardized testing reports. Incidents of student misbehavior have been on the rise due to a lack of a consistent and effective school-wide discipline policy.

Compounding these problems is a lack of leadership with vision. Strategic planning has been abandoned over the past several years. The school's mission statement hasn't been updated in those years. Teachers work in isolation of each other without a commonly held belief system about teaching and learning. In sum, teachers and parents want the school to flourish and are hopeful that this new experienced principal, with an excellent reputation based on his previous work in similar schools, can turn the school around.

This chapter has shared ongoing and recent research into the important of relationship building to enable a school to flourish. What ideas can you cull from this research that would enable Bernard Davies to affect the changes necessary so that the school can flourish? The chapter provided several steps that need to be taken. Can you take the general principles from the fields of positive psychology and positive organizational scholarship, as discussed in the chapter, to provide practical, concrete steps and actions that Mr. Davies can employ to transform the school into a flourishing one? Discuss as many leadership and managerial strategies that could be employed to assist the new principal to accomplish his goal. More specifically, what are some implications of the concept of "well-being" in terms of managing, not just leading a school?

REFERENCES

Bakker, A. B. (2008). The work-related flow inventory: Construction and initial validation of the WOLF. *Journal of Vocational Behavior, 72*(3), 400–414. https://doi.org/10.1016/j.jvb.2007.11.007.

Bakker, A. B., & Schaufeli, W. B. (2008). Positive organizational behavior: Engaged employees in flourishing organizations. *Journal of Organizational Behavior, 29*(22), 147–154. https://doi.org/10.1002/job.515.

Barth, R. S. (2006). Improving relationships within the schoolhouse. *Educational Leadership, 63*(6), 8–13.

Cameron, K. S. (2012). *Positive leadership: Strategies for extraordinary performance.* Berrett-Koehler.

Cameron, K. S., Mora, C., Leutscher, T., & Calarco, M. (2011). Effects of positive practices on organizational effectiveness. *The Journal of Applied Behavioral Science, 47*(3), 266–308. https://doi.org/10.1177/0021886310395514.

Carr, A. (2004). *Positive psychology: The science of happiness and human strengths.* Routledge.

Cherkowski, S., Hanson, K., & Walker, K. (2018). *Mindful alignment: Foundations of educator flourishing.* Lexington.

Cherkowski, S., Kutsyuruba, B., & Walker, K. (2020). Positive leadership: animating purpose, presence, passion and play for flourishing in schools. *Journal of Educational Administration, 58*(4), 401–415. https://doi.org/10.1108/jea-04-2019-0076.

Cherkowski, S., & Walker, K. (2013). Living the flourish question: Positivity as an orientation for the preparation of teacher candidates. *Northwest Journal of Teacher Education, 11*(2), 80–102. https://doi.org/10.15760/nwjte.2013.11.2.5.

Cherkowski, S., & Walker, K. (2016). Purpose, passion and play. *Journal of Educational Administration, 54*(4), 378–392. https://doi.org/10.1108/jea-10-2014-0124.

Clarke, P. (2000). *Learning schools, learning systems.* Continuum.

Colbert, A. E., Bono, J. E., & Purvanova, R. K. (2016). Flourishing via workplace relationships: Moving beyond instrumental support. *Academy of Management Journal, 59*(4), 1199–1223. https://doi.org/10.5465/amj.2014.0506.

Cooperrider, D. L. (2013). The spark, the flame, and the torch: The positive arc of systemic strengths in the appreciative inquiry design summit. In D. L. Cooperrider and M. Avital (Eds.), *Organizational generativity: The appreciative inquiry summit and a scholarship of transformation* (pp. 211–248). Emerald. https://doi.org/10.1108/s1475-9152(2013)0000004008.

Creswell, J. W. (2014). *Research design: Qualitative, quantitative, and mixed methods approaches* (4th ed.). Sage.

Dodge, R., Daly, A., Huyton, J., & Sanders, L. (2012). The challenge of defining well-being. *International Journal of Well-being, 2*(3), 222–235. https://doi.org/10.5502/ijw.v2i3.4.

Duckworth, A. L., Peterson, C., Mathews, M. D., & Kelly, D. R. (2007). Grit: Perseverance and passion for long term goals. *Journal of Personality and Social Psychology, 92*(6), 1087–1010. https://doi.org/10.1037/0022-3514.92.6.1087.

Dutton, J. E., Glynn, M. A., & Spreitzer, G. M. (2006). Positive organizational scholarship. In J. Greenhaus & G. Callahan (Eds.), *Encyclopedia of Career Development* (pp. 641–644). Sage.

Dutton, J. E., & Spreitzer, G. M. (2014). *How to be a positive leader: Insights from the leading thinkers on positive organizations.* Berrett-Koehler.

Fredrickson, B. L., Arizmendi, C., & Van Cappellen, P. (2021). Same-day, cross-day, and upward spiral relations between positive affect and positive health behaviours. *Psychology & Health, 36*(4), 444–460. https://doi.org/10.1080/08870446.2020.1778696.

Fredrickson, B. L., & Losada, M. F. (2005). Positive affect and the complex dynamics of human flourishing. *American Psychologist, 60*(7), 678–686. https://doi.org/10.1037/0003-066X.60.7.678.

Gable, S. L., & Haidt, J. (2005). What (and why) is positive psychology? *General Psychology, 9*(2), 103–110. https://doi.org/10.1037/1089-2680.9.2.103.

Harter, J. K., Schmidt, F. L., & Keyes, C. (2003). Well-being in the workplace and its relationship to business outcomes: A review of the Gallup studies. In C. Keyes & J. Haidt (Eds.), *Flourishing: Positive psychology and the life well-lived* (pp. 205–224). American Psychological Association. https://doi.org/10.1037/10594-009.

Haybron, D. (2008). Happiness, the self and human flourishing. *Utilitas, 20*(1), 21–49. https://doi.org/10.1017/S0953820807002889.

Hayward, K., Pannozzo, L., & Colman, R. (2007). *Developing indicators for the educated populace domain of the Canadian Index of Well-being.* Atkinson Charitable Foundation.

Keyes, C. (2002). The mental health continuum: From languishing to flourishing in life. *Journal of Health and Social Behavior, 43*(2), 207–222. https://doi.org/10.2307/3090197.

Keyes, C. (2003). Complete mental health: An agenda for the 21st century. In C. Keyes & J. Haidt (Eds.), *Flourishing: Positive psychology and the life well-lived* (pp. 293–312). American Psychological Association.

Keyes, C. (2016). Why flourishing? In D. W. Harward (Ed.), *Well-being and higher education* (pp. 99–108). Bringing Theory to Practice.

Keyes, C., & Annas, J. (2009). Feeling good and functioning well: Distinctive concepts in ancient philosophy and contemporary scienc. *American Psychologist, 6*(2), 95–108. https://doi.org/10.1080/17439760902844228.

Kim, G. J. (2016). *Happy schools: A framework for learner well-being in the Asia Pacific*. United Nations Educational, Scientific and Cultural Organization

Kutsyuruba, B., Kharyati, T., & Arghash, N. (2021). Exploring the sense of flourishing among Canada's Outstanding Principals. In K. Walker, B. Kutsyuruba, & S. Cherkowski (Eds.), *Positive leadership for flourishing schools* (pp. 231–252). Information Age Publishing.

Kutsyuruba, B., & Walker, K. (2021). *The lifecycle of trust in education: Leaders as moral agents*. Edward Elgar.

Langley, S. (2012). Positive relationships at work. In S. Roffey (Ed.), *Positive relationships: Evidence based practice across the world* (pp. 163–180). Springer.

Leithwood, K., Harris, A., & Strauss, T. (2010). *Leading school turnaround: how successful leaders transform low-performing schools*. Jossey-Bass.

Leithwood, K., & McAdie, P. (2007). Teacher working conditions that matter. *Education Canada, 47*(2), 42–45.

Louis, K. S., & Murphy, J. F. (2018). The potential of positive leadership for school improvement: A cross-disciplinary synthesis. *Nordic Journal of Comparative and International Education (NJCIE), 2*(2–3), 165–180. https://doi.org/10.7577/njcie.2790.

Lyubomirsky, S., King, L., & Diener, E. (2005). The benefits of frequent positive affect: Does happiness lead to success? *Psychological Bulletin, 131*, 803–855.

Martin, A. J., & Marsh, H. W. (2006). Academic resilience and its psychological and educational correlates: A construct validity approach. *Psychology in Schools, 43*(3), 267–281. https://doi.org/10.1002/pits.20149.

Mishra, A. K., & Mishra, K. E. (2013). *Becoming a trustworthy leader: Psychology and practice*. Routledge.

Nelson, S. K., Layous, K., Cole, S. W., & Lyubomirsky, S. (2016). Do unto others or treat yourself? The effects of prosocial and self-focused behavior on psychological flourishing. *Emotion, 16*(6), 850–861.

Noble, T., & McGrath, H. (2015). PROSPER: A new framework for positive education. *Psychology of Well-Being, 5*(2), 1–17. https://doi.org/10.1186/s13612-015-0030-2.

Patterson, J. L., Goens, G. A., & Reed, D. E. (2009). *Resilient leadership for turbulent times: A guide to thriving in the face of adversity*. Rowman & Littlefield.

Quinn, R. W., & Quinn, R. E. (2015). *Lift: The fundamental state of leadership*. Berrett-Koehler.

Roberts, L. M., & Dutton, J. E. (2009). *Exploring positive identities and organizations: Building a theoretical and research foundation*. Routledge.

Roffey, S. (2007). Transformation and emotional literacy: The role of school leaders in developing a caring community. *Leading and Managing, 13*(1), 16–30.

Roffey, S. (2008). Emotional literacy and the ecology of school well-being. *Educational & Child Psychology, 25*(2), 29–39.

Roffey, S. (2012). Developing positive relationships in schools. In S. Roffey (Ed.), *Positive relationships: Evidence based practice across the world* (pp. 145–162). Springer. https://doi.org/10.1007/978-94-007-2147-0_9.

Scarnati, J. T. (2002). Leaders as role models: 12 rules. *Career Development International, 7*(3), 181–189. https://doi.org/10.1108/13620430210414892.

Sekerka, L. E., Vacharkulksemsuk, T., & Fredrickson, B. L. (2011). Positive emotions: Broadening and building upward spirals of sustainable enterprise. In K. S. Cameron & G. M. Spreitzer (Eds.), *The Oxford handbook of positive organizational scholarship* (pp. 168–177). Oxford University Press.

Seligman, M. E. P. (2011). *Flourish: A visionary new understanding of happiness and well-being*. Simon and Schuster.

Seligman, M. E. P., Ernst, R., Gillham, J., Reivich, K., & Linkins, M. (2009). Positive education: Positive psychology and classroom interventions. *Oxford Review of Education, 35*, 293–311. https://doi.10.1080/03054980902934563.

Seligman, M. E. P., Steen, T. A., Park, N., & Peterson, C. (2005). Positive psychology progress: Empirical validation of interventions. *American Psychologist, 60*(5), 410–421. https://doi.org/10.1037/0003-066X.60.5.410.

Sin, N. L., & Lyubomirsky, S. (2009). Enhancing well-being and alleviating depressive symptoms with positive psychology interventions: A practice-friendly meta-analysis. *Journal of Clinical Psychology, 65*(5), 467–487. https://doi.org/10.1002/jclp.20593.

Spreitzer, G. M., Sutcliffe, K., Dutton, J. E., Sonnenshein, S., & Grant, A. M. (2005). A socially embedded model of thriving at work. *Organization Science, 16*(5), 537–549. https://doi.org/10.1287/orsc.1050.0153.

The Learning Partnership. (2019). *Canada's outstanding principals*. https://www.thelearningpartnership.ca/programs/canadas-outstanding-principals.

Tschannen-Moran, M., & Clement, D. (2018). Fostering more vibrant schools. *Educational Leadership, 75*(6), 28–33.

VanderWeele, T. J., McNeely, E., & Koh, H. K. (2019). Reimagining health—flourishing. *JAMA, 321*(17), 1667–1668. https://doi:10.1001/jama.2019.3035.

Walker, K., Kutsyuruba, B., & Cherkowski, S. (Eds.). (2021). *Positive leadership for flourishing schools*. Information Age Publishing.

Wheatley, M. J. (1999). Bringing schools back to life: Schools as living systems. In F. M. Duffy & J. D. Dale (Eds.), *Creating successful school systems: Voices from the university, the field, and the community* (pp. 3–19). Christopher-Gordon.

Wilderom, C. P. M. (2011). Toward positive work cultures and climates. In N. M. Ashkanasy, C. P. M. Wilderom, & M. F. Peterson (Eds.), *The handbook of organizational culture and climate* (2nd ed., pp. 79–84). Sage.

Chapter Eight

Fiscal Management

Guidelines for School Leaders

Leonard H. Elovitz

INTRODUCTION

Education in the United States is big business. Total expenditures for the 2016–17 school year for public elementary and secondary schools were reported at $739 billion (listed in 2018–19 dollars). This amounts to $14,439 per student enrolled in public schools in the fall of 2018, which broke down as follows: current expense = $12,794, capital outlay = $1,266, and debt service = $379 (U.S. Department of Education, 2020). A similar situation arises when one examines finances at a district level.

The local school district is very likely the biggest business in its community, and it often has the most employees engaged in the various functions of the educational enterprise. It is therefore incumbent upon school leaders to be conversant with the financial aspects of running the district and its schools. Because those who manage fiscal matters are responsible for the acquisition and expenditure of so much public money, they have a fiduciary responsibility to make sure that the funds are being handled legally and efficiently and in the best interest of the taxpayers. Today's educational leaders also have a professional and moral obligation to the students and their parents to make financial decisions that support an educational program that maximizes learning opportunities and provides for the best possibility for student success.

This chapter explores the financial skills necessary for school leaders to be successful at both the district and school levels. Even though the discussion focuses on the United States, the general principles apply to most school contexts globally. The chapter begins with a look at sources of revenue (where the money comes from), followed by planning for expenditures (how the money is allocated), and purchasing (how the money is spent). There will also be some ideas for reallocating resources and identifying possible supplemental sources of revenue.

WHERE DOES THE MONEY COME FROM?

It is incumbent upon school managers to be conversant with the ways schools are funded generally and specifically given the unique context of each school/district. The U.S. Constitution is silent when it comes to education; therefore, education has become a function of the states under the provisions of the 10th Amendment. But this does not mean that there is no federal involvement in the enterprise. There have been many court cases involving schools. Most frequent are disputes involving Article I, Section 10, and the 1st, 5th, and 14th Amendments (Reutter & Hamilton, 1970).

When it comes to school finance, 49 of the 50 states consider the funding of schools to be a joint effort between the states and the local school districts. Only Hawaii has a fully state-funded system (Thompson & Marlow, n.d.). However, the Federal Government assists and/or influences education through several grants approved for distribution by the U.S. Congress. It is generally accepted that federal aid should not be used in place of state and local funding.

It is interesting to see how much revenue has been contributed to school districts by the three governmental levels over the years. Table 8.1 lists that breakdown from selected school years shown in thousands of dollars (U.S. Department of Education, 2018). There are other sources of revenue such as

Table 8.1. Revenues for public elementary and secondary schools, by source of funds (current dollars in thousands)

School Year	Federal	State	Local	Total
1919–20	$2,475	$160,085	$807,561	$970,121
1929–30	7,334	353,670	1,727,553	2,088,557
1939–40	39,810	684,354	1,536,363	2,260,527
1949–50	155,848	2,165,689	3,115,507	5,437,044
1959–60	651,639	5,768,047	8,326,932	14,746,618
1969–70	3,219,557	16,062,776	20,984,589	40,266,922
1979–80	9,503,537	45,348,814	42,028,813	96,881,164
1989–90	12,700,784	98,238,633	97,608,157	208,547,573
1999–00	27,097,866	184,613,352	161,232,584	372,943,802
2009–10	75,997,858	258,863,973	261,528,833	596,390,664
2014–15	55,002,853	301,529,692	291,146,585	647,679,130
2015–16	55,981,180	318,572,978	303,824,317	678,378,476

Table 8.2. Percentage distribution of revenues for public elementary and secondary schools, by source of funds

School Year	Federal	State	Local
1919–20	0.26%	16.5%	83.2%
1929–30	0.4%	16.9%	82.7%
1939–40	1.8%	30.3%	68.0%
1949–50	2.9%	39.8%	57.3%
1959–60	4.4%	39.1%	56.5%
1969–70	8.0%	39.9%	52.1%
1979–80	9.8%	46.8%	43.4%
1989–90	6.1%	47.1%	46.8%
1999–00	7.3%	49.5%	43.2%
2009–10	12.7%	43.4%	43.9%
2014–15	8.5%	46.6%	45.0%
2015–16	8.3%	47.0%	44.8%

private grants, donations, and rentals. However, these contributions are minor in comparison to governmental funding.

Table 8.2 and Figure 8.1 show the above data by percentage of contribution.

Over the past century, the major portion of educational funding switched dramatically from local to state sources. In the 1919–20 school year, the local district accounted for 83.2% of district revenues whereas the state provided 16.5%. More recently in 2015–16, the state share increased to 47.0%, and the

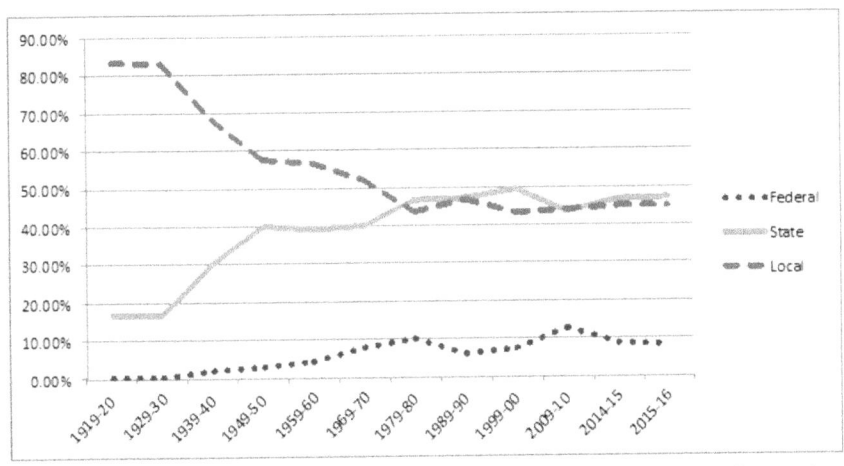

Figure 8.1. Percentage distribution of revenues for public elementary and secondary schools by source of funds.
Source: Author created using data from the Digest of Educational Statistics: https://nces.ed.gov/programs/digest/d18/tables/dt18_235.10.asp.

local district decreased to 44.8%. The upside to the local taxpayer is quite obvious. However, there is a downside. With increased funding comes the demand for increased control, which tends to erode grassroots decision-making. The federal contribution started out to be very small in 1919–20 and before. More recently it has grown somewhat to around 10%.

Although the federal share of educational funding is small, there is little doubt that the U.S. Government has had a major influence on the nation's schools. Congress derives its powers to influence education from Article 1 under the requirements to provide for a strong national defense and to promote the general welfare. Federal funding largely comes in the form of categorical grants which can be an entitlement, based on the number of qualifying pupils (i.e., Title I), or competitive, based on the approval resulting from an application process. There are also less restrictive block grants that cover a wide range of areas. It is important to note that, in general, federal funding is meant to supplement rather than supplant funding by the other levels of government.

As previously indicated, education is a function of the states and, as such, they are responsible for the development and maintenance of their public education systems. The state as a higher level of government than the local district can better ensure the availability of an adequate system of education. It can also take advantage of a much larger tax base.

The states' contributions come mostly in the form of state aid, which is determined by a legislated complex formula. State aid can be general, which comes with few restrictions on how the funds are utilized. The aid can also be categorical, addressing certain needs, students, or areas of operation. Some examples include special education, transportation, school building aid, and particular projects.

Each state collects funds mainly through a system of taxation determined by their legislatures. The major sources include individual income taxes and sales taxes followed by several other levies and funding sources. The combination of these sources of revenue is unique to the individual states.

The application of the state aid formula is the process through which the state transfers funds to the local school districts. Around the beginning of the twentieth century, the states began to take more of an interest in the funding of schools. The history of the evolution from simple systems like matching grants and flat grants to current formulas that attempt to address adequacy, equity, efficiency, and liberty is interesting, but beyond the scope of this chapter.

In most cases, the greatest portion of revenue at the school district level is generated by local property taxes. It behooves the school administrator to be knowledgeable about the impact of the school system on local tax bills. The amount to be raised by local property tax for school purposes is calculated by subtracting all other funding from the planned expenditures in the budget. For example, a school district's budgeted (planned) expenditures total $10,000,000. It receives $2,000,000 in state aid, $500,000 in federal aid, and another $500,000 from other miscellaneous revenues. The school district must raise $7,000,000 in local taxes to balance the budget. Because most of the funding comes from the combination of state aid and property taxes, generally, the higher the aid, the lower the tax rate.

The tax rate for school purposes is determined by dividing the amount to be raised by local taxes by the total assessed valuation of the real property in the district. Let's say that a district has a total assessed valuation of $350,000,000. Dividing that amount into the $7,000,000 that the district needs, results in a tax rate for school purposes of 0.02 (or 2% or $2.00 per $100 of assessed valuation). Taxpayers in a community want to know, "What is the proposed budget going to cost?" Generally, the answer can be determined by simply multiplying the tax rate by the assessed valuation of the property and house on it. If we use the above rate of 2.0% or $2.00 per $100 of assessed valuation on a house and property assessed at $200,000 the calculation would be:

Taxes Owed = Tax Rate x Assessed valuation
Taxes Owed = .02 x $200,000
Taxes Owed = $4,000

The application of the tax rate calculation can become a little more complicated when the school budget year goes from July 1st to June 30th and the tax year runs from January 1st to December 31st. Building and district administrators must be conversant with the particulars of revenues for educational purposes as they pertain to their situation.

HOW IS THE MONEY ALLOCATED?

One of the most important functions of the school district leader who oversees fiscal matters is to develop a budget that meets the needs of the students and the community. At the building level, principals must often do the same with the funding allocated to their buildings. The budget is essentially a one-year blueprint for the receipt and disbursement of funds to meet the goals and objectives of the school district. It generally goes through an approval process, and once approved, ideally reflects the wishes of the community. Depending on the applicable statutes, a proposed budget is developed by the superintendent of schools for presentation and approval or modification by the board of education. The proposed budget is subject to approval by the state. It must then gain the approval of the community either through a public vote or a review by another local body such as a council or a board of school estimate.

As a first step in the one-year budget cycle, it is important to determine to examine the planning process. A key element of that process is to determine who will be involved and what their roles should be. In a centralized system of decision-making, the flow is from the top-down, with the superintendent and central office staff making most of the decisions. In a decentralized system, the flow is from the bottom up, with stakeholder committees at the school level involved in the planning process to varying degrees. In reality, this is more of a continuum than a dichotomy. Modern management theory would have the district lean toward the decentralized end, being careful to involve individuals who have the knowledge and interest to be productive members of the process.

The next step should be a needs assessment based on the last step of the prior year's cycle, which is an evaluation of how well the district and the individual schools performed in meeting the goals and objectives during the previous academic year. These goals and objectives are often derived from a multi-year strategic plan. As a result of this assessment, decisions should be made on the continuation, modification, replacement, and or abandonment of the previous goals and objectives. This process is complicated by the fact that this part of the planning process begins before the current fiscal year has been completed.

Sadly, the evaluation process is too often ignored or given little attention during the budgeting process. Too often, the lazy administrator utilizes the incremental methodology of budget development: that is simply adding the same percentage of increase or decrease to each budget line of the current year's budget. This approach is often employed because it is easy to accomplish and to understand. The district and building administrators justify this methodology by telling critics that it treats everyone fairly. However, due to the lack of attention to any educational plan, the students often lose out.

Another popular methodology that is closely aligned with incremental is line-item budgeting which again, uses the current budget as the base and makes increases or decreases to major budget categories such as salaries or teaching supplies. Here the percentage of change may be based on things like negotiated salary settlements and anticipated inflation. The line items may also be broken down into subcategories to provide better specificity. For example, salaries can be broken down into instructional and non-instructional, and further, instructional can be broken down into elementary and secondary.

Line-item budgeting, particularly in larger districts, can be formula-driven, where major district functions like transportation and building maintenance are budgeted centrally at the district office, and individual school allocations are determined on a formula often based on anticipated enrollment. The district might decide that for budgetary purposes it wants to maintain a student to teacher ratio of 20:1. Therefore, if the projected enrollment at a school is for an increase of 100 students, the budget might allow for the hiring of 5 additional teachers, depending on the distribution of the additional students. Likewise, if the projection calls for a decrease of 100 students, the budget line could be reduced proportionately. A formula based on anticipated enrollment can also be applied to other budget lines such as textbooks and teaching supplies.

Using a formula approach often results from a high degree of centralization, leaving the principals and their staffs with little if any say in the decision-making process. The line-item methodology can be somewhat more complex than incremental and remains popular because it is easy to understand. However, it does not give much consideration to how the previous budget helped the district and schools meet their goals and objectives.

Budgets built in the ways illustrated above can be recast into a program format by spreading the amounts on the appropriation lines over the various programs of the district. The listings are still attributed to the appropriate lines as they apply to each program. In that way, comparisons can be made between the various district programs. A program budget can answer questions such as, "How much are we spending for textbooks in social studies, and how does that compare with the amount spent for language arts?" The programs can further be broken down by school to answer similar types of questions. Generally, the cost per pupil is calculated for each program to make the comparisons more meaningful. There is a caveat to be aware of if personnel costs are included in determining the program costs. Teacher salary schedules are often tied to longevity. If the social studies department is staffed by veteran teachers and the science department by relatively younger teachers, the cost per pupil would likely be much higher for social studies.

The budget can also be built in this way by having the schools submit budget requests in a program format. Those appropriations can then be easily totaled along the appropriate lines to provide the line budget for the schools and the entire district. This program budgeting system (PBS) provides for more decentralized control. The programming, planning, and budgeting system (PPBS) is a major step up from PBS in that it requires that there be an educational action plan that indicates the goals and objectives that are consistent with the district's strategic plan for each program and how they will be met in the upcoming budget year. This planning process involves the weighing of alternatives and the ascribing of costs to the agreed-upon activities.

Still another step up involves the addition of the process of evaluation. The methodology now becomes programming, planning, budgeting, and evaluation systems (PPBES). Under this system, the budgeting process begins with an evaluation of how well the educational units met or are meeting the previous and current goals and objectives. Decisions then need to be made as to whether to keep, modify, or abandon those goals and/or objectives and their accompanying action plans. This process should result in a modified educational action plan, the costs of which are determined and included in the proposed program budget. These activities and decisions are best made at the building level under the direction of the principal.

Zero-based budgeting (ZBB) is in direct opposition to incremental and line-item methodologies. In its purest application, the current year's budget is completely zeroed out and the district starts from scratch. There is no guarantee that a budget item will survive from year to year. Appropriations for the planned year have to be newly justified, and alternatives for reaching educational goals and objectives are considered. This methodology forces an annual evaluation of programs and must involve the participation of teachers and other staff members. The most significant disadvantage is that it can be very time-consuming.

Under building-based or site-based budgeting (SBB), decisions are made closer to the actual process of education. In this form of decentralized management, decision-making power is given to a committee of representative stakeholders usually chaired by the school principal. In many cases, community members are also asked to participate. The power of the committee is constrained by legal requirements and district guidelines. The committee is usually given budgetary authority over objects including teaching supplies, textbooks, school activities, equipment, and non-instructional supplies. Budget matters dealing with salaries and benefits of personnel are usually left to the central office along with areas like transportation, food service, maintenance, capital outlay, and debt service. SBB is more consistent with current thinking about organizational management. It does have some drawbacks, however. It is time-consuming and could result in animosity when one program is pitted against another as members of the management team seek to maximize the levels of funding for their departments or grade levels.

In actuality, the system that a district decides to use to develop its budget is usually an amalgamation of parts of the above methodologies. Presented below is a possible sequence of steps in a process that does just that:

1. Determine an approximate percentage increase that might be acceptable. This factor is reached by the superintendent and central office staff after evaluating the economic climate, estimating sources of revenue, and consulting with the board of education.
2. Complete enrollment projections for each building and grade. Project course enrollments for middle schools and high schools.
3. Determine a percentage of increase or decrease of the per-pupil budget allocations for the schools and apply those changes to the current building budget bases. Generally, the base will be highest at the high schools, followed by the middle schools and the elementary schools.
4. Develop the building budget base for each school by multiplying the new per pupil base amount by the projected number of students. The base is the total amount that each school is provided to be distributed over the programs and lines over which the site-based committee has been given authority.
5. Central office provides principals with their base amounts and projected enrollments.
6. Central office provides principals with program budget sheets that list, by budget line, expenditure amounts from the previous year, appropriation amounts for the current year, and blanks for the coming year.
7. Principals meet with their site-based committees and subcommittees to complete their assessment of how well their school is doing on meeting their goals and objectives and to determine the goals and objectives and action plans for the upcoming year.
8. The projected costs are plugged into the program sheets. Modifications are made to make sure that the school total does not exceed the building budget base. The school-based committee may also develop proposals in the form of decision packets for program changes or additions that are too costly to include in their bases.
9. Principals submit completed budget requests and decision packets for expenditures beyond the base.
10. Principals and other purchase center heads meet with the superintendent and selected central office administrators to defend their budget requests.
11. Items inside the building budget base are reviewed and approved.
12. Decision packets are presented and approved, modified, or rejected.
13. Approved appropriations are folded into the district's proposed budget.
14. That budget is then presented to the board of education and moves through the process of approval consistent with district regulations and state statutes.

It is apparent that a process like the one above leans heavily on PPBES and SBS, but it also includes elements taken from the other methodologies. Once a district decides on its methodology, the steps and responsibilities should be translated into a budget development calendar.

Around 80% of a school district's budget is expended on personnel salaries and benefits. The degree of control granted to the schools in a site-based management system varies and is controlled by state statutes and regulations, district policies and regulations, and the results of collective bargaining. Generally, even in the most modern school system, the central office maintains a modicum of control over the decisions involving the budgeting of personnel.

Initially, the cost of the implementation of the salary guides should be calculated by moving each staff member up a step. Known anticipated horizontal moves based on changes in training levels should be figured in as well as anticipated retirements and reductions in force. If the district is in negotiations, a reasonable salary increase should be included for planning purposes. Personnel changes that result from program modifications, additions, and/or deletion need to be considered in the calculations.

Probably the biggest driving force behind personnel budgeting is the projected student enrollment. It is necessary to have a clear idea of anticipated student enrollment and distribution. An excellent discussion of enrollment projection methodologies can be found in *School district master planning: A practical guide to demographics & facilities planning* (Carey, 2011). School districts usually have a class size policy, which will guide how many classes and sections will be needed. Once this is determined, it is an easy set of calculations to determine what appropriations could be folded into the proposed budget.

Appropriations for physical plant needs are generally handled centrally. However, the principal and building budget committee should take a tour of the building with the district administrator in charge of facilities to determine a prioritized list of needs. These lists are then reviewed at the central office, and a prioritized list of projects with related costs is developed for the district.

Similar processes are employed with the administrators and supervisors of other district functions including special education, technology, curriculum and instruction, transportation, food service, etc. The key is to make sure that past performance on the goals and objectives is evaluated and that decision-making is participatory. Once the appropriations for each purchase center are approved, all of the program sheets are combined into a preliminary line budget for further approvals by the board, the state, and usually by the taxpayers.

When the preliminary budget is not approved, reductions have to be made. The possible processes utilized are similar to those of budget development:

- Incremental—all lines reduced by the same percentage
- Line Item—lines are reduced by determined amounts that add up to a reduction
- Formula—budget reductions based on a formula usually driven by enrollment
- PPBES—Objectives and their funding are delayed or eliminated, or action plans are modified
- ZBB—Decision packets are prioritized into proposed cuts
- SBB—Principal is given an amount to cut, and he or she determines, along with the site-based committee, how to modify their budget requests

HOW IS THE MONEY SPENT?

The district now has a blueprint for expenditure that has been approved and is consistent with the goals and objectives of the district's educational plan. A new school year begins, and it is time to spend the funds. The expenditure of school funds is strictly controlled by statute and code, and district procedures must be in compliance. The business office of the school district generally develops purchasing guidelines for the schools and other purchase centers to use. These rules should be drawn to assist in the educational process, not to hinder it.

Purchasing should be on a cycle, a system that ensures orders are placed, filled, and paid for on time. Districts generally use purchase orders to acquire goods and services. Consideration should be given to just how many signatures are necessary for approval before the orders are sent out. If the proposed purchase is consistent with the approved budget and the district guidelines, and there are funds remaining in the appropriate budget lines, there is little reason not to send a purchase order out. It is incumbent on the building administrators to make sure that the purchase that they are requesting is valid before sending in the order.

The process for a principal to request a budget transfer to cover a purchase that would overdraw an account should be easy as long as there is still money available in other building accounts. Educational decisions of this nature should not be overruled by the business office. Once the items are received or the services are completed, the business office should be notified in a timely fashion so that payments can be processed. This usually involves the filing of a receiving copy of the purchase order or some sort of verification in a digitized system. The principal or other school manager assigned should oversee this function. Vendors should be able to expect payment soon after they have completed their end of the transaction.

EXPANDING RESOURCES

As funding from traditional sources becomes harder to count on, school administrators are seeking alternative forms of revenue. Creative school officials have come up with some very novel ways of raising money. An important caveat when considering alternative funding sources is to be sure that any such plans are consistent with state statutes and regulations. It is also necessary to consider district policies and regulations.

There are many examples of smaller school districts sharing services in areas like maintenance, transportation, business office operations, athletics, etc. Combining school districts through regionalization is often proposed to expand student services and reduce administrative costs. There are also examples of districts that have room in their facilities seeking to increase their enrollments and funding by recruiting students from outside the district and charging tuition for attendance.

Another source of additional revenue is the charging of participation fees in areas like extracurricular activities and sports, summer school, field trips, music lessons, etc. There is also the possibility of charging for textbooks and supplemental materials such as laboratory supplies. Because education is a state function guaranteed by the individual constitutions, there has been a number of lawsuits surrounding a school district's right to impose such fees. The results of these cases have been mixed (King et al., 2003). Also raised are policy and administrative issues in areas such as the parents' ability to pay, the manner in which money is to be collected, and a possible reduction in student participation.

School facilities rentals are common. Many districts allow community groups to use the buildings at little or no rental fee. Some charge just for pro-rated costs for utilities and custodial services. A different schedule of costs is often developed for groups outside the community. The district might want to consider actively recruiting outside commercial enterprises to rent school space during evenings and on weekends.

Advertising in schools is an interesting area. Many school districts have policies that strictly prohibit any form of advertising because students are a captive audience. Some do permit the selling of ads in yearbooks and student performance programs to help offset the costs of these publications. Some districts get some revenue from allowing advertising at school athletic facilities during games, on school walls, on school buses, and even on athletic uniforms.

School fundraising has long been a staple. PTAs and booster groups sponsor tricky trays, raffles, band candy, bake sales, etc. Some school districts have opted to consolidate their fundraising by establishing private foundations to provide general support or funding for specified educational projects. Because federal laws and state statutes regulate non-profit charitable organizations, it is important to have legal guidance before proceeding. An excellent discussion of foundations can be found in *School finance: Achieving high standards with equity and efficiency* (King et al., 2003).

Numerous examples of partnerships with industry can be found. They include programs that augment fundraising, provide mentoring and tutoring, sponsor and/or provide professional development, provide management expertise, student internships, and job experience, etc. Businesses are willing to invest because they recognize that they have a stake in a well-educated and prepared future workforce. Colleges also find it advantageous to partner with public schools. A major example is advanced placement, where students can gain college credit for courses delivered by a high school. There are also examples of direct arrangements where high school students can earn credits for classes taken at nearby colleges or for courses offered at their high school. In the area of teacher preparation, there are numerous examples of colleges and districts coming together to provide professional development schools.

Public and private grants can also provide additional revenue to schools, and/or school districts. State and federal grants might be formula-driven, making allocations based on the number of students that meet a set of criteria, or they may be competitive, where awards are made based on responses in an application. There are some private foundations and individuals that provide funding for programs of special interest to them. School leaders need to keep abreast of the possibilities in these areas and pursue funding that fits in with their educational plan.

It is important to reemphasize that these types of external funding should be used to augment the district's budget and not to replace revenues collected to run the basic programs. Some school districts employ a grants administrator to seek out opportunities and to assist the district and schools in applying for and implementing funded programs. Others might assign the duties to an existing administrator or a part-timer.

CONCLUSION

This chapter provides a primer of sorts to ensure that administrators and supervisors are keenly aware of their fiscal management responsibilities. One final note is important to emphasize. School leaders should constantly be evaluating their decisions to reallocate resources to get equal or better results for less money. "We've always done it this way" is a very poor excuse when faced with declining revenues. There are many examples in the literature of schools and districts meeting the challenge by making minor to radical changes to how they spend money.

As indicated earlier, most of the budget is expended on personnel salaries and benefits. In *The secret of TSL: The revolutionary discovery that raises school performance,* Ouchi (2009) discusses how a number of schools, given the management authority, reallocate their budgets to better meet their goals. In *Every child, every day: A digital conversion model for student achievement,* Edwards (2014) tells the story of how his school district was able to increase student performance through a greater reliance on technology. Several examples of repurposing expenditures can be found in Odden and Archibald's (2001) *Reallocating resources: How to boost student achievement without asking for more.*

In the 21st century, during the continued era of increased accountability and dwindling resources, it is incumbent upon school leaders to be knowledgeable and resourceful in how they acquire funding as well as allocate and expend it in the best interest of their students.

CASE STUDY

You are a newly hired superintendent of schools in a large urban district that has not been successful in meeting the needs of its students. The district has a poor history in regard to fiscal management and budget approval. In fact, the two previous superintendents and business administrators were fired for incompetency. Specifically, their lack of knowledge of the varied budgeting processes and their inability to monitor the process efficiently led to their demise, so to speak. Given, the various ideas expressed in this chapter, describe, in detail, answers to these questions:

1. What initial steps would you take to begin to turn things around?
2. What steps would you take to develop a budget that meets the needs of the students and the community?
3. Would you utilize line-item budgeting? Why or why not?
4. What other budgeting strategies might you consider?
5. What challenges might you anticipate in getting the budget approved?
6. In what ways might you expand financial resources for the district?

REFERENCES

Carey, K. D. (2011). *School district master planning: A practical guide to demographics & facilities planning.* Rowman & Littlefield.

Edwards, M. A. (2014). *Every child, every day: A digital conversion model for Student achievement.* Pearson.

King, R. A., Swanson, A. D., & Sweetland, S. R. (2003). *School finance: Achieving high standards with equity and efficiency* (3rd ed.). Pearson.

Odden, A., & Archibald, S. (2001) *Reallocating resources: How to boost student achievement without asking for more.* Corwin.

Ouchi, W. G. (2009). *The secret of TSL.* Simon and Schuster.

Reutter, E. E., & Hamilton, R. R. (1970). *The law of public education.* The Foundation Press.

Thompson, J. A., & Marlow S. E. (n.d.). *Hawaii.* National Center for Education Statistics. https://nces.ed.gov/edfin/pdf/StFinance/Hawaii.pdf.

U.S. Department of Education, National Center for Education Statistics (2018). *Revenues for public elementary and secondary schools, by source of funds: Selected years, 1919–20 through 2015–16.* https://nces.ed.gov/programs/digest/d18/tables/dt18_235.10.asp.

U.S. Department of Education, National Center for Education Statistics (2020). *Expenditures.* https://nces.ed.gov/fastfacts/display.asp?id=66.

Chapter Nine

Best Practices in School Management
A Multi-Dimensional Perspective
Jeffrey Glanz

INTRODUCTION

As one peruses the history of school management globally and the most influential theorists, one realizes that, for the most part, educators viewed management as distinct from leadership, at least in terms of function (Kaya et al., 2011; Rao & Hari Hara Raju, 2015). Some even viewed leadership as a "higher calling" than school management (Alvy & Robbins, 2005). Many noticed that in the past several decades, management, as a term, if not a function, received little attention (Craig, 2020). As we entered the new century however, a clear shift in thinking became apparent. "Successful new and veteran principals alike . . . view their managerial role as vital to their leadership responsibilities" (Alvy & Robbins, 2005, p. 52).

There were, of course, forward-thinkers who saw them as complementary. Sergiovanni (2000), early on, viewed management and leadership as co-dependent processes. More recently, Shaked and Schechter (2020) see schools as complex organizations that require managerial and leadership expertise. The point is that educators in the 21st century, building on these prior conceptions, understand that schools today are too complex to bifurcate the two processes (Connolly et al., 2019). Contributors to this volume likewise view them as complementary.

Since it is widely acknowledged that managerial functions are vital to a principal's success, this chapter would like to outline in broad strokes many, albeit not all, of the important tasks school managers must grapple with, and in doing so integrate some of the ideas in the previous chapters. The chapter will discuss *four areas* crucial for managers to address (Glanz, 2006):

1. Managing the school organization
2. Coordinating and overseeing school facilities
3. Highlighting school budget issues
4. Managing human relations

Although this is not meant as an exhaustive treatment of the subject, it does cover the main elements every school manager should address. Thus, the focus in this chapter is viewing school management from a multi-pronged approach. Neglect in one area will have ramifications for other areas. Therefore, a holistic or multi-dimensional approach is necessary.

One last caveat, though. The chapter serves as a conclusion of sorts to this volume and as it attempts to draw upon ideas culled from previous chapters, it will be written in an almost topical, list format. Such an approach accomplishes two things. One, it makes for easy reading, and two, more importantly, since this book is meant to focus on the realities that principals and other school leaders face daily it offers practical guidelines, mostly in the form of questions for consideration. This volume, after all, is part of the Rowman & Littlefield School Leadership Series meant to draw upon extant research or theories in the field to offer practical suggestions for school leaders.

AREA 1: MANAGING THE SCHOOL ORGANIZATION

Any book on management, school-related or otherwise, highlights the critical importance of organizational skills in terms of managing an organization. School management in the 21st century is particularly challenging given the ever-increasing social, economic, technological, and educational challenges confronting principals. Without effective and efficient skills of organization, a leader will be quickly subsumed with a myriad of important and urgent issues that need attention. Planning and setting up organizational mechanisms, therefore, are imperative. Beyond, establishing school-wide organizational frameworks to deal with inevitable challenges leaders face, personal organizational skills are equally essential (Kraft et al., 2016; Wellisch et al., 1978).

Literature and real-life cases demonstrate that sometimes intelligent, creative, and well-meaning administrators fail to "get things done" because of their inability to juggle responsibilities, multi-task competing exigencies, or simply organize priorities to get everything done. For instance, the literature also indicates that some of these individual leaders can focus exceedingly well on one particular task. They often spend an inordinate time getting everything perfect, and in the end, they do. But while focusing on one important managerial task, several other necessary tasks are neglected. Other leaders are simply disorganized, not because of laziness or unwillingness. Some leaders are very creative. Getting their activities or plans organized is difficult. Unless they compensate for their lack of organizational skills, they often fail to achieve their goals.

Based on extant research, literature, and practice three critical aspects related to organizing personal and school matters follow that if attended to will go a long way to managing a school efficiently and effectively.

1. *Establish a School-Wide System for Organization* (Thoonen et al., 2012):
    a. Is there a system (a pre-determined set of rules and procedures) to manage the school, in general, and the main office, in particular?
    b. Is there a master schedule/calendar prominently posted in the school and on the website?
    c. Is there a written and widely disseminated plan for when a school-wide emergency occurs?
    d. Are there formalized, clear communications networks designed to disseminate information efficiently?
    e. Is there a system in place to screen incoming regular office mail that includes sorting and prioritizing emails?
    f. Is there a checks and balances system to ensure responses are accurate and timely?
    g. Are there a set of written goals and objectives (both personal and school-related)?
    h. Based on these goals and objectives, are daily, weekly, and monthly to-do lists developed aligned to and for each goal or objective?
    i. Is there an evaluative mechanism to ensure that office personnel competently perform their respective duties?
    j. Is technology and concomitant applications employed to ensure efficiency in various aspects of managing school operations?
    k. Do school personnel (including staff, teachers, and other administrators) feel secure in knowing that things are running smoothly on an average day as well as when crises or issues arise because there is a system in place for dealing with such exigencies?
2. *Personal Organization Skills* (Francis et al., 2019):
    a. Have the school leaders assessed the degree to which they are personally organized?
    b. Have mechanisms been put into place to make up for any personal deficiencies in terms of personal organizational management?

    c. Is a plan in place for delegation of various tasks, if necessary?
    d. What kind of assistance might the leader need to help with personal organization skills?
3. *Managing Time* (Grissom et al., 2015):
    a. How might the leader determine that maximum efficiency in time-related matters exists?
    b. Who assesses efficient management of time in the school?
    c. Is a timetable established to ensure successful completion of the various important projects?
    d. Do school leaders build think-time into their schedules?
    e. How do leaders know that meetings are conducted efficiently and effectively?

In conclusion, organizational skills are fundamental to success. It is the first thing to consider in managing a school. School leaders must assess themselves based, in part, on the questions above to determine their level of efficiency as well as the overall organizational effectiveness. Periodic and yearly evaluations should occur to assess the degree to which the school is organized in such a way as to maximize human and material resources.

AREA 2: COORDINATING AND OVERSEEING SCHOOL FACILITIES

Ideally, the school plant including all facilities should be influenced by the school's educational program. Unfortunately, the educational program must often accommodate to existing facilities. Let's look at a case in which the program must align itself with existing structures. A new principal, for example, is eager to employ a progressive educational program that includes bridge-classes to facilitate inclusionary practices. Such a program requires co-joined classrooms. The school facility had not been renovated for forty years. Therefore, the principal's plans either need revising or school renovations may be necessary.

    Another management issue in regard to school facilities is that safety, security, comfort, and adaptability should be considered in plant and facilities management. Plans need to be collaboratively developed for the proper management of the plant and its facilities, supplies, and equipment. Ongoing evaluation of educational needs and services is needed to determine the extent to which the physical facilities, supplies, and equipment are meeting these needs (Lunenburg, 2010).

Here are some key questions principals should ask about general facilities management:

a. Is there a written, articulated, and shared plan for use of the school facilities?
b. Are teachers and staff solicited about the use of school space in the building?
c. Is space utilization efficient?
d. Does the plan consider the use of the building during after-school hours, and how that might affect normal functioning during the day?
e. How is surplus space used for maximum efficiency?
f. Is there a plan for periodic inspection of all facilities?
g. Given the use of technology, is the school safely wired and maintained?
h. Is there effective communication with the local fire department, police, etc.?
i. Is safety part of the school's curriculum?
j. Are storage rooms inspected for safety and fire violations?

Based on these initial sample questions, four critical aspects related to facilities should be monitored.

1. *Coordinating School Safety and Security* (Stader, 2012):
   a. Are the physical characteristics and structures conducive to ensuring safety in all parts of the building?
   b. Are all areas of the building sufficiently lit?
   c. Have all potential trouble spots been identified and remedied?
   d. Are safety signs strategically placed throughout the building and surrounding premises?
   e. Are school safety guards supervised?
   f. Has a school climate survey been developed, distributed, and analyzed yearly?
   g. Are there clear school-wide rules and procedures for general behavior?
   h. Is there a systematic plan to evaluate school safety?
2. *Overseeing the Cafeteria* (DeRoche, 1987):
   a. Is there a formal policy for programming lunch periods?
   b. Has the cafeteria environment been assessed regarding size, location, resources, etc.?
   c. Have seating routines been established and reviewed?
   d. Have the staff been prepared to manage all aspects of cafeteria management?

e. Have indoor versus outdoor lunch procedures been established and reviewed?
   f. Are games and other activities planned for indoor lunches?
   g. Is there a procedure to monitor and reply to student reactions to food and other facilities in the cafeteria?
3. *Working with the Custodial Staff* (DeRoche, 1987):
   a. Are cooperative agreements with the custodial staff in place?
   b. Are there ongoing meetings with the custodian to ensure contractual obligations are met?
   c. Are mechanisms in place to mediate conflicts between teachers and custodial staff?
   d. Are measurable goals for custodial staff in place?
   e. Is an evaluation plan established?
   f. Are there planned walk-around to oversee the entire building and grounds bi-weekly?
4. *Conducting a Facilities Audit: What should be included?* (Whitaker, 1995):
   a. Physical structure, classrooms, offices, computer labs, restrooms, play-areas, all equipment, etc.
   b. Health standards, heating systems, plumbing, ventilation, etc.
   c. Safety regulations
   d. Communications systems and equipment
   e. Aesthetic appearance of building
   f. Efficient use of energy
   g. Space conducive for instructional purposes
   h. Access for students with disabilities
   i. School-wide wireless capacity

In conclusion, good managers realize the impact of the physical environment on learning and student achievement.

AREA 3: HIGHLIGHTING SCHOOL BUDGET ISSUES

More common in the 21st century than in the previous ones, is the fact that school budgets are hierarchically driven. Often Ministries or Boards of Education dictate budgets based on a variety of factors unique to each school. In some places, principals are left to their resources to create budgets for approval by a board. Still, in other places, it's a combination in terms of negotiating for school funds.

Regardless of the situation, there are key factors to consider in handling a budget. There are essential knowledge and skills necessary that can be learned from a mentor, seminar, etc. Here are some areas to attend to:

a. Understand the budget-making process
b. Develop a budget in consultation with faculty and staff
c. Prepare a budget that addresses all instructional needs
d. Keep accurate financial records of receipts and expenditures
e. Prepare accurate reports for audits and reporting to various constituents in an ongoing fashion
f. Manage and evaluate budget allocations

Below is a list of questions to consider:

a. Is the principal familiar with the budget classification system of the school or district?
b. What are the basic budget categories?
c. Has the principal involved faculty and staff in the budget process?
d. Has the principal aligned the budget based on the current strategic plan?
e. Is the leader familiar with line-item budgeting?
f. How can technology assist in planning and monitoring the budget?
g. Has the principal made a compelling case to higher authorities for increases in budget allocations for the school?
h. Once the budget has been allocated, how will the principal ensure equitable and fair distribution of funds?
i. What accounting procedures have been set in place?
j. Is the principal familiar with competitive bidding regulations?
k. How will the budget process be evaluated and by whom?
l. Have competent staff been assigned to oversee various aspects of the budget and the auditing process?

In conclusion, school budgeting is a laborious yet essential process. Most principals, especially inexperienced ones, need additional assistance in this aspect of school management. Leaders should be encouraged to attend district workshops and seminars on budgeting and other finance-related issues. A close professional relationship with the district chief financial officer is imperative.

AREA 4: MANAGING HUMAN RELATIONS

The needs of the individual and the school organization must be balanced (Bolman & Deal, 2017). Bolman and Deal's classic guiding principles include, among others, that organizations exist to serve human needs. Both the organization and the individual are mutually co-dependent. Human beings have emotional, psychological, and social needs that must be supported by the organization.

Keeping these principles in mind, the school manager needs to meet the requirements of the organization so that the school accomplishes its objectives, but, at the same time, be mindful of the needs of humans for stability and growth. An annual assessment of school climate is imperative (MacNeil et al., 2009). This area is worthy of a book in its own right. Here we will briefly address just three aspects:

1. Providing ongoing professional development for faculty (Glanz, 2012):
   a. Improving the supervisory knowledge and skills of principals and their assistants based on cutting-edge technologies in instructional leadership that are intended to improve teaching practice.
   b. Developing a school-wide professional development plan aimed at improving classroom-based instruction by focusing on teaching practices and curricular processes so that all students achieve appropriate levels of performance.
   c. Incorporating other instructional leadership initiatives such as action research, peer coaching, critical friends, meaningful walk-throughs, all of which deepen the school's commitment to a culture of instructional excellence.
2. Evaluating personnel and programs (Sanders & Sullins, 2005):
   a. As a school leader, one is committed to ensuring the highest standards of professional behavior via accountability. Principals must ensure that students are being taught by competent professionals. Therefore, a fair, equitable, and collaborative set of evaluative measures need to be established. Danielson's (2013) model is among the most popular systems available.
   b. Principals as managers must ensure that all school programs, instructional or otherwise, are effective and meeting their objectives. Principals as managers need to know how to employ rigorous program evaluative measures, both formatively and summatively.
3. Dealing with Conflict (Larasati & Raharja, 2019):
   a. School managers realize that conflicts and disagreements are natural occurrences in all organizations. Managers need knowledge and skills in conflict resolution strategies so that conflicts are aired fairly and resolved reasonably. Depending on the situation, managers must be ready to make adjustments in scheduling or in general management procedures to accommodate for differences among people.

CONCLUSION

The theme of this chapter, and the book as a whole, has been to indicate a comprehensive way of thinking about school management in the 21st century. Certainly, many ideas expressed in this chapter and volume were as relevant in the 20th century as they are today. Yet, a fundamental premise in this work is that although similarities in school management are time universal, there are stark and urgent differences in the way present-day school leaders need to manage their schools. Schools in the 21st century will continue to undergo transformational changes technologically, for instance, as well as encounter crises (e.g., pandemics) that have not been experienced since the early 1900s. Given these facts, leaders need to consider the best ways to manage their schools to provide for efficient and effective school operations.

Another major distinction based on this chapter and book relates to a change in viewing school management. A perusal of older works and practices on the subject indicates that principals, for instance, cannot solely devote themselves to serving as managers. Yesteryear, principals perceived themselves first and foremost as managers with little attention to, for example, instructional leadership. Principals were often selected based only on previous experiences related to managing operations, even if their prior work as a manager was not in a school. Conversely, others relegated management of a school as a necessary cumbersome task that needed attention, but the emphasis was to be placed primarily on other administrative or leadership objectives, such as visioning, public relations, instructional supervision, and the like.

Our emphasis here is to indicate that both are crucial for the work of school leaders in the 21st century. Principals must affirm that both leadership and management are essential to achieve success in all facets of running a school. One is not necessarily more important than the other. An instructional leader cannot effectuate positive results without mindful attention to areas of management that support instructional goals and objectives. Principals who only view their roles as managers will often neglect other very important leadership-based school initiatives.

In this light, schools need to hire principals who, at once, realize the import of both functions, and have the requisite skills and experiences that support best practices in, for example, instructional leadership and school management. Some refer to this conception as seeing the two as two sides of one coin. Others see them as two halves of a one-sided coin. I prefer the latter metaphor because it communicates more starkly the co-dependent nature of both.

This chapter has tried to present school management viewing its various facets multi-dimensionally. It has also tried to impart some practical guidelines in the form of questions, primarily, to support the work of 21st-century principals. The case study that follows attempts to encourage readers to apply some of the ideas expressed in this chapter.

CASE STUDY

Jason Nutley, a former sales manager for a large marketing firm, decided to change careers in his early thirties. "Although I was a good manager and interacted with people often, I felt unsatisfied in terms of making a real difference in the lives of others," he explained at his first public school teaching job interview. He had obtained a master's degree in teaching while still working for his marketing firm. Although he worked long hours, he set aside two evenings a week to obtain his degree. He was hired, while in his late 20s, as a 12th-grade teacher. After a few years, he realized that education provided him the most satisfaction. In the evenings, again, he undertook a second master's degree in educational leadership, and by his early 30s, he was ready to make a move to school administration. Highly motivated and excited, he applied for a principalship. "I knew," Jason explained, "that going from a position as a teacher to a principal is a big leap. But I figured my years as a sales manager might suffice, so I applied for this position."

During the interview, the panel asked him many questions, including these:

1. You have managed people at a marketing company. What makes you think that those skills are transferable to managing a school?
2. Do you see a difference between school management and school leadership? Explain.
3. Since your school-related experiences are limited, would you consider delegating some instructional leadership tasks to someone else, like your vice principal, so you can focus mainly on managing school operations?
4. What do you see as the main challenges you will face as a principal in terms of both school management and leadership?
5. What specific strategies might you employ in the following areas?:
   a. School organization
   b. Facilities management
   c. Finance and budget
   d. Human resources management
   e. School communications
   f. Personnel management

Question: How would you answer these questions posed to Mr. Nutley?

REFERENCES

Alvy, H., & Robbins, P. (2005). Growing into leadership. *Educational Leadership, 62*(8), 50–54.

Bolman, L. G., & Deal, T. E. (2017). *Reframing organizations: Artistry, choice, and leadership.* Jossey-Bass.

Connolly, M., James, C., & Fertig, M. (2019). The difference between educational management and educational leadership and the importance of educational responsibility. *Educational Management, Administration & Leadership 47*(4), 504–519.

Craig, I. (2020). Whatever happened to educational management? The case for reinstatement. *Management in Education, 35*(1), 52–57. https://doi.org/10.1177/0892020620962813.

Danielson, C. (2013). *The framework for teaching evaluation instrument.* The Danielson Group.

DeRoche, W. F. (1987). *An administrator's guide for evaluating programs and personnel: An effective schools approach* (2nd ed.). Allyn and Bacon.

Francis, O.B., & Oluwatoyin, F.C. (2019). Principals' personnel characteristic skills: A predictor of teachers' classroom management in Ekiti State Secondary School. *International Journal of Educational Leadership and Management, 7*(1), 72–103. http://dx.doi.org/10.17583/ijelm.2019.3573.

Glanz, J. (2006). *What every principal should know about operational leadership.* Corwin.

Glanz, J. (2012). *Improving instructional quality in Jewish day schools and yeshivot: Best practices culled from research and practices in the field.* The Azrieli Papers.

Grissom, J. A., Loeb, S., & Mitani, H. (2015). Principal time management skills: Explaining patterns in principals' time use, job stress, and perceived effectiveness. *Journal of Educational Administration, 53*(6), 773–793. https://doi.org/10.1108/JEA-09-2014-0117.

Kaya, I., Habaci, I, Küçük, S., Sivri, M., & Adigüzelli, F. (2011). Historical development of educational management. *World Applied Sciences Journal, 15*(3), 392–399. https://www.idosi.org/wasj/wasj15(3)11/13.pdf.

Kraft, M., Marinell, W. H., & Yee, D. (2016). Schools as organizations: Examining school climate, teacher turnover, and student achievement in NYC. *Research Alliance for New York City Schools.*

Larasati, R., & Raharja, S. (2019). *Conflict management in improving school effectiveness.* 3rd International Conference on Learning Innovation and Quality Education.

Lunenburg, F. C. (2010). School facilities management. *National Forum of Educational Administration and Supervision Journal, 27*(4), 1–7. http://www.nationalforum.com/Electronic%20Journal%20Volumes/Lunenburg,%20Fred%20C.%20School%20Facilities%20Management%20V27%20N4%202010.pdf.

MacNeil, A. J., Prater, D. L., & Busch, S. (2009). The effects of school culture and climate on student achievement. *International Journal of Leadership in Education, 12*(1), 73–84. doi:10.1080/13603120701576241.

Rao, M., & Hari Hara Raju, K. (2015). Management education: A historical perspective. *International Journal of Academic Research, 2*(8), 71–78. http://ijar.org.in/stuff/issues/v2-i2(8)/v2-i2(8)-a012.pdf.

Sanders, J. R., & Sullins, C. D. (2005). *Evaluating school programs: An educator's guide.* Corwin.

Sergiovanni, T. J. (2000). *Leadership for the schoolhouse.* Jossey-Bass.

Shaked H., & Schechter C. (2020). Systems thinking leadership: New explorations for school improvement. *Management in Education, 34*(3), 107–114. https://doi.org/10.1177/089202062090732.

Stader, D. (2012). *Leadership for a culture of school safety: Linking theory to practice.* Rowman & Littlefield.

Thoonen, E. E. J., Sleegers, P., & Peetsma, T. (2012). Building school-wide capacity for improvement: The role of leadership, school organizational conditions, and teacher factors. *School Effectiveness and School Improvement, 23*(4), 1–20. https://doi.org/10.1080/09243453.2012.678867.

Wellisch, J., MacQueen, A., Carriere, R., & Duck, G. (1978). School management and organization in successful schools (ESAA In-Depth Study Schools). *Sociology of Education, 51*(3), 211–226. https://doi.org/10.2307/2112666.

Whitaker, M. J. (1995). Conducting a facility management audit. *Facilities, 13*(6), 6–12. https://doi.org/10.1108/02632779510085159.

Index

Bourdieu, P., 65–66; Notions of "habitus" and "field," 66–67; Notions of social capital, 67–69

COVID-19 pandemic, 37, 38, 41, 44, 45, 52, 60, 61, 92

Dewey, John, 8, 15, 20

Fiscal management, 109–110; Budgeting, 113–119; Expanding resources, 120–121; Expenditures, 119; Source of funding, 110–113
Fullan, Michael, 11, 12, 20, 30, 33

Kozol, Jonathan, 12–13

Leaders: As fiscal managers, 109, 110, 113–114, 116, 119, 121–122; As moral agents, 7–8; Dealing with legal issues, 79; Free speech, 82–85; Meta-leaders, 25–28
Leadership: Adaptive, 30, 33; As a concept, 7; For flourishing, 93–94; Instructional, 25–28; Principal leaders vs. principal as manager, 1–3, 20, 23, 30, 31, 133, 134; Schools as moral institutions, 8–13; With a moral purpose, 7, 10; Managing change, 12, 20, 24–25, 30–31, 42, 64, 70, 79, 125, 133; Suggestions for, 30–31

McGregor, Douglas's Theories X and Y, 29, 33
Moral leadership: Practical applications of, 14–19

Plato: Criticism of technology, 38–39
Principal and schools: As an effective leader, 25; As instructional leader, 2; Building relationships, 101–103; COP (Canada's Outstanding Principals) program, 4, 94, 96, 101, 102, 107

Reverse management, 29–30

Schools: As communities, 12; As moral institutions, 8–10; As organizations, 2, 4, 7. 67, 80, 93, 103, 125–126, 131; As systems, 93–94; Classic theories, 28–29; Culture, 8, 10, 15, 17, 30, 31, 65, 69, 95, 98, 101, 103, 132; Culture of care, 100; Decentralization in NYC, 13–14; Flourishing, 94–95, 97–101; Well-being, 93, 94, 95, 96, 101, 102, 105, 106, 107

School management: And school leadership, 1–2; And school safety, 69–71; Conceptions of, 2, 51; Contrast to school leaders, 1, 125; Early conceptions of, 23; Fiscal, 109–110; Managing budget, 119, 130–131; Managing facilities, 128–130; Managing human relations, 131–132; Managing organization, 126–128; Managing safety, 63; Practical suggestions for, 42–43; Principles of boundary management, 69–71; Trust building, 26, 53, 57, 68, 70, 77, 98, 99, 102, 103, 106

School managers: And technology, 38; Practical suggestions, 42–43, 126–132

Social media, 82–85

Taylor, Frederick W., 28, 29, 35

Teacher autonomy, 25–29, 67, 69, 77

Teacher development, 15, 19, 34, 44, 61; Professional development opportunities, 40, 41, 42, 46

Teacher evaluation: And school improvement, 52–53; As a discipline, 52; Formative and summative, 53; Practical guidelines, 55–57; Principles of, 52–55; Quality vs. evaluation, 51; Self-evaluation, 54

Technology, 82, 86; ICT (Information & Communication Technology), 37; Digitized technologies, 39, 119; Integration of, 38; Positive culture towards, 40; Practical applications, 42–43; Post-Pandemic conditions of ICT integration, 40; TAM (Technology Acceptance Model), 39–41; TPACK (Technology Pedagogical Content Knowledge), 41–41

Title VII, 79–82

Title IX, 79, 86–90

About the Editor & Contributors

Jeffrey Glanz is Professor and Head of the M.Ed. program in Leadership and Management in Educational Systems at Michlalah Jerusalem College. He held the Silverstein Endowed Chair in Professional Ethics and Values and was a tenured professor of Education and Administration at the Azrieli Graduate School of Yeshiva University. He was Dean of Graduate Studies and Chair of Education at Wagner College in Staten Island, New York. He was executive assistant to the president at Kean University and at Kean was named Graduate Teacher of the Year by the Student Graduate Association. He was also the recipient of the Presidential Award for Outstanding Scholarship. He was a teacher and school administrator in New York City for 20 years. Prof. Glanz has authored, co-authored, edited, and co-edited 22 books on various educational topics, including four books with Rowman & Littlefield Publishers: (1) *Revisiting Dewey: Best Practices for Educating the Whole Child Today* (2010, co-authored with Daniel Stuckart); (2) *Action Research: An Educational Leader's Guide to School Improvement* (2014, author); (3) *Supervision: New Perspectives for Theory and Practice* (2015, co-edited with Sally Zepeda); and (4) *Crisis and Pandemic Leadership: Implications for Meeting the Needs of Students, Teachers, and Parents* (2021, editor). yosglanz@gmail.com; www.jeffreyglanz.com

Köksal Banoğlu has recently received his double doctorate degree in Educational Sciences from Ghent University and in Educational Management and Supervision from Marmara University. He has taught graduate and undergraduate courses in various universities in Istanbul, Turkey. Some of his research interests are technology leadership, organizational learning, school health, and applied statistics. His more recent research orientation revolves around applying probabilistic/inferential social network analysis (SNA) approaches to the investigation of school managers' technology leadership practices, teachers' professional learning interactions and children's peer aggression/bullying behaviors in school settings. koksal_banoglu@hotmail.com

Pascale Benoliel is Senior Lecturer and faculty member at the Faculty of Education in the Leadership, Organizational Development and Policy Program at Bar-Ilan University, Israel. Her research focuses on issues pertaining to educational policies and school leadership. She is focusing on global education governance, cross-cultural and comparative research combining quantitative and qualitative research. Also, Dr. Benoliel investigates how the interplay between individual and environmental factors may influence the attitudes and behaviors of both principals, school management team members, and school faculty with implications for school effectiveness. Her studies have focused on team leadership, boundary management, participative leadership and systems thinking within the educational context. She has received several awards, including the Outstanding Reviewer in the 2020 Emerald Literati Awards for Excellence and the Highly Commended Award Winner of the 2012 Emerald/EFMD Outstanding Doctoral Research Awards in the Education and Leadership strategy category. pascale.benoliel@biu.ac.il

Clair T. Berube is Assistant Professor of Education, Virginia Wesleyan University. Dr. Berube received her Ph.D. in Urban Studies/Education from Old Dominion University. She also has a B.A. in Psychology from Virginia Wesleyan University and a B.S. and MSED in Education from Old Dominion University. Her research areas include urban schools, the effects of high stakes testing on learning, gender and race in STEM education and problem-based learning. Dr. Berube has experience with grants and with teacher preparation at all levels. She is the author of several articles and books, including a new release entitled *The Investments: An American Conspiracy* (Information Age Publishers, 2020). She loves science, including physics and theoretical physics; psychology including how people learn, and social justice topics in education. Dr. Berube has won teaching awards both at the public school and University levels. cberube@vwu.edu.

Maurice R. Berube, Eminent Scholar Emeritus, Old Dominion University is a well-known scholar of educational leadership, policy, and politics. Dr. Berube holds a Ph.D. in Education from Union Graduate School, M.A. from New York University, and a B.A. from Fordham University. He held the distinction of Eminent Scholar of Educational Leadership at Old Dominion

University, and was Assistant Professor at Queens College, CUNY where he worked with Marilyn Gittell in the Urban Studies Department. This work resulted in an important civil rights book titled *Confrontation at Ocean-Hill Brownsville* which documented the work he and others did for the Community Control Movement. This was mentioned in the documentary "Eyes on the Prize." Dr. Berube was also Chief of Research and Information for the Department of Education, New York City Mayor's Office, under Mayor Lindsey. He has published books on the roles of presidents in education, unions, and educational reform. mberube@odu.edu.

Leonard H. Elovitz is currently Adjunct Professor in the College of Education and Human Services at Seton Hall University in South Orange, NJ. After a distinguished career as a school district administrator, he was employed as an Associate Professor in the Department of Educational Leadership at Kean University in Union, NJ. As chair of that department, he designed and implemented the Ed.D. program in Urban Leadership. After 17 years, he retired from that position in 2016. He has authored many articles in national and state professional journals and presented at a number of conferences. In 2015, he co-authored a book titled, *Quantitative Data Analysis Using Microsoft Excel: A School Administrator's Guide*, which was followed by the Mac edition in 2016. Dr. Elovitz received his Bachelor's and Master's from Montclair State University and a Doctorate in the Administration of Educational Programs from Teachers College, Columbia University. lenelovitz@gmail.com

Sedat Gümüş is Associate Professor of Educational Administration in the Department of Educational Policy and Leadership at the Education University of Hong Kong, Hong Kong SAR. His research interests include comparative and international education, educational leadership, and higher education. His most recent research focuses on the relationship among leadership practices, teacher behaviors, and learning in schools. He currently serves on the advisory board of Bridging Theory and Practice: The Rowman & Littlefield School Leadership Book Series, as well as undertakes editorial responsibilities in several academic journals. gumussed@gmail.com

Helen M. Hazi is a Professor Emerita of Educational Leadership at West Virginia University and was a teacher, a Supervisor of Curriculum and Instruction, a curriculum specialist, and an expert witness. She is the founder of the Supervision and Instructional Leadership AERA-SIG. Dr. Hazi writes about legal issues that have a consequence for the discourse communities of supervision in books and journals such as the *Journal of Educational Supervision*,

Journal of Staff Development, and *Educational Policy Analysis Archives*. Recent topics include teacher evaluation instruments, statutes, litigation, and marketing; professional development; and instructional improvement. hmhazi@verizon.net; https://helenhazi.faculty.wvu.edu

Benjamin Kutsyuruba is Associate Professor in Educational Leadership, Policy, and School Law in the Faculty of Education at Queen's University. Throughout his career, Benjamin has worked as a teacher, researcher, manager, and professor in the field of education in Ukraine and Canada. For 10 years, he served as an Associate Director of Social Program Evaluation Group (SPEG) at Queen's University. His research interests include educational policymaking; educational leadership; induction, mentorship and development of teachers; trust, moral agency, and ethical decision-making in education; international education; school climate, safety, well-being, and flourishing; and educational change, reform, and restructuring. His current research projects focus on positive leadership, flourishing in schools, educator well-being, and teacher induction and mentoring in international settings. ben.kutsyuruba@queensu.ca

R. Stewart Mayers is Professor and Chair of the Department of Educational Instruction and Leadership and Director of Teacher Education at Southeastern Oklahoma State University. His research interests include legal issues in employee and student social media usage and transgender rights in public schools. His research has been published in such journals as the *Brigham Young University Education and Law Journal, the Clearing House*, and *Journal of Cases in Educational Leadership*. The Education Law Association published his monograph, *Social Media, Public Schools, and the Law*. He has authored/coauthored four book chapters and three books. He currently serves on the Professional Partnership/Legal Literacy Committee of the Education Law Association. smayers@se.edu

Michael Reichel is a Lecturer in the Leadership and Management in Educational Systems at Michlalah Jerusalem College. He was a school administrator in Jewish elementary and middle schools for over 20 years in the United States as well as presently the Principal of the Chorev elementary school for boys in Jerusalem, Israel. His research interests include management leadership, theories in educational administration, bridging theory with practice in educational administration programs, and recruitment strategies for hiring qualified principals. He is currently conducting a major study on the latter issue. He is also an ordained orthodox rabbi and has published a manuscript on Persian American Jews. Rmreichel@hotmail.com

Shmuel Shenhav is Head of the Graduate School of Education at Michlalah Jerusalem College, in Bayit Vegan, Jerusalem, Israel, Head of the Avney Rosha Program for the training of school leaders in the Israel Ministry of Education, and Head of the National-Religious Center for Leadership in Israel. He served as a school principal for many years. He is a national speaker on issues related to educational leadership and has published in journals such as the *International Journal of Educational Reform*. shenhav@huji.ac.il

www.ingramcontent.com/pod-product-compliance
Lightning Source LLC
Chambersburg PA
CBHW052051300426
44117CB00012B/2067